Science
interact

● **Key Stage 3 Science**

7

Alison Alexander

Helen Harden

Jenny Versey

DL **D**YNAMIC
LEARNING
Innovate • Motivate • Personalise
CD-ROM INSIDE

HODDER
EDUCATION
PART OF HACHETTE LIVRE UK

Although every effort has been made to ensure that website addresses are correct at time of going to press, Hodder Education cannot be held responsible for the content of any website mentioned in this book. It is sometimes possible to find a relocated web page by typing in the address of the home page for a website in the URL window of your browser.

Hachette's policy is to use papers that are natural, renewable and recyclable products and made from wood grown in sustainable forests. The logging and manufacturing processes are expected to conform to the environmental regulations of the country of origin.

Orders: please contact Bookpoint Ltd, 130 Milton Park, Abingdon, Oxon OX14 4SB. Telephone: (44) 01235 827720. Fax: (44) 01235 400454. Lines are open 9.00 – 5.00, Monday to Saturday, with a 24-hour message answering service. Visit our website at www.hoddereducation.co.uk

© Alison Alexander, Helen Harden, Jenny Versey 2008
First published in 2008 by
Hodder Education,
part of Hachette Livre UK,
338 Euston Road,
London NW1 3BH.

Impression number   5   4   3   2   1
Year   2012   2011   2010   2009   2008

Cover photo: green tree frog, David M. Schleser/Nature's Images/Science Photo Library
Illustrations by Oxford Designers and Illustrators Ltd
Typeset in 12/14pt Clearface by Stephen Rowling/Springworks
Printed in Italy

A catalogue record for this title is available from the British Library

ISBN: 978 0 340 94897 2

Contents

Acknowledgements		4
Welcome to *Science Interact*		5
	1 Life under the microscope	6
	2 Elementary	18
	3 Big ideas	27
	4 Life goes on	41
	5 Volcanoes	54
	6 Ready, steady, go	64
	7 Life and environment	76
	8 Acid attack!	86
	9 Charges on the move	96
Index		107

Acknowledgements

The Publishers would like to thank the following for permission to reproduce copyright photographs in this book:

p.6 *t* D. P. Wilson/FLPA/Minden Pictures, *c* Visuals Unlimited/Corbis, *bl* Breck P. Kent/Photolibrary.com, *br* Philippe Psaila/Science Photo Library; **p.7** It Stock RM/Photolibrary.com; **p.8** Collection CNRI/Phototake Science/Photolibrary.com; **p.9** CDC/PHIL/Corbis; **p.11** *l* Photodisc, *r* Science Source/Science Photo Library, **p.12** Sean Cayton/The Image Works/www.topfoto.co.uk; **p.13** Clouds Hill Imaging Ltd/Corbis; **p.15** Jack K. Clark/the Image Works/www.topfoto.co.uk; **p.16** *c* Bettmann/Corbis, *b* Scott Camazine/Alamy; **p.17** Dr Hans Gelderblom/ Visuals Unlimited/Getty Images; **p.20** Visual Arts Library (London)/Alamy; **p.25** *t* IBM Research, Almaden Research Center, *l* Aleksandr Lobanov/ iStockphoto.com; **p.26** *l* Imperial War Museum, *r* Sean Sprague/Still Pictures; **p.28** *t, cl* NASA, ESA, S. Beckwith (STScl) and the HUDF Team, *cc* NASA Jet Propulsion Laboratory (NASA_JPL), *cr* NASA-JPL/Caltech/Steve Golden, *bl* Dennis diCicco/Corbis, *bc* Tomasz Gzell/epa/Corbis, *br* STScl/NASA/Corbis; **p.30** akg-images/Erich Lessing; **p.33** *t* Andi Duff/Alamy, *c* Endolith/flickr (licensed under a Creative Commons Attribution 2.0 Licence), *b* Roger Ressmeyer/ Corbis; **p.34** *all* Cordelia Molloy/Science Photo Library; **p.38** *t* Martyn F. Chillmaid, *bl* Wolfram Schroll/zefa/Corbis, *bc* Ted Pink/Alamy, *br* Chris Howes/Wild Places Photography/Alamy; **p.39** *l* Paul Rapson/Science Photo Library, *lc* Hodder Archive, *rc* Amy Trustram Eve/Science Photo Library, *r* Jason Bye/ Alamy; **p.41** Thierry Berrod, Mona Lisa Production/Science Photo Library; **p.42** *t* CNRI/Science Photo Library, *b* Hodder Archive; **p.47** *t* TEK Image/ Science Photo Library, *c* Mark Thomas/Science Photo Library; **p.50** *l* www.topfoto.com, *r* BSIP, Astier/Science Photo Library; **p.51** Blend Images/Punchstock; **p.52** Micro Discovery/Corbis; **p.53** The Garden Picture Library/Alamy; **p. 56** *tl* Joyce Photographics/Science Photo Library, *tr* Corbis, *b* Chris Howes/Wild Places Photography/Alamy; **p.58** *l* Robert Chapek/Index Stock Imagery/photolibrary.com, *r* Johnny Bouchier/Red Cover/Getty Images; **p.59** *both* Last Resort Picture Library; **p.60** Mark Sykes/Alamy; **p.61** US Geological Survey (USGS); **p.63** US Geological Survey Photograph by Dave Harlow 12 June 1991; **p.64** Craig Lovell/Corbis; **p.66** *tl* Najlah Feanny/Corbis, *bl* Yoav Levy/Phototake Science/photolibrary.com, *cl* Photodisc/Getty Images, *cr* Richard R. Hansen/Science Photo Library, *far r* Visuals Unlimited/Corbis; **p.67** www.tomdodson.co.uk/www.studioarts.co.uk; **p.68** Jack Sullivan/Alamy; **p.69** Chris Simpson/Cordaiy Photo Library Ltd/Corbis; **p.70** *www.andphotos.com*; **p.71** VOSA; **p.72** *l* Tony Marshall/Empics Sport/PA Photos, *r* Duomo/Corbis; **p.73** *tl* Jose Fuste Raga/Corbis, *cl* Peter Steiner/Alamy, *r* Kuttig-People/Alamy; **p.74** Ray Tang/Rex Features; **p.80** Biosphoto/Cancalosi John/Still Pictures; **p.81** *t* Photodisc, *c* Tom Brakefield/Corbis; **p.82** Biosphoto/Gasco Nicolas/Still Pictures; **p.83** CSI Productions/Alamy; **p.84** *t* Nic Hamilton/Alamy, *c* Andrew Darrington/Alamy; **p.85** John Carey/photolibrary.com; **p.86** Martyn F. Chillmaid; **p.88** Charles D. Winters/Science Photo Library; **p.91** INSADCO Photography/ Alamy; **p.94** Rob Cousins/Alamy; **p.100** *t* NASA, *b* Leslie Garland Picture Library/Alamy; **p.103** Andrew Lambert Photography/Science Photo Library; **p.104** www.cycom.co.uk

Every effort has been made to trace all copyright holders, but if any have been inadvertently overlooked the Publishers will be pleased to make the necessary arrangements at the first opportunity.

Welcome to *Science Interact*

In this book you will find all the key science information you need, and lots more besides.

Your teacher may ask you to do some of the questions and activities. These will help check that you have understood things, and may make you think a bit more about what you have been learning. Some will help you improve your investigative skills and some will help you find out about other scientists' experiments and discoveries.

If you have a computer available to you, insert the CD-ROM into the CD-ROM drive. When it has loaded, go to the Contents and click on the topic you want to look at. You should then find it easy to bring up on screen the pages you are interested in. Move the mouse about and you will see that the different parts of the page become 'live'. Where there is a CD symbol on the page, this means that the CD-ROM has something extra that is not on the page of the book. This could be an illustration or an animation to help you understand something you may find difficult. It could be something to save you time with your homework such as a letter outline, or some suggested web pages to use as a starting point for research. It could be some extra information which may be useful, especially if your home isn't full of science books!

If you want to take things further, check out some of the ideas and information on the CD-ROM about the wide range of career possibilities involving science.

Good luck and good experimenting!

Life under the microscope

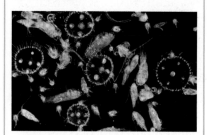

Here are some examples of microbes. On the CD-ROM you can see some others and read about the different types of microbes.

● Plankton magnified ×5

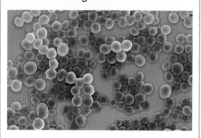

● Bacteria magnified ×50 000

Microscopic things

The world is teeming with living things that we call **microscopic**. This means they are so small they can only be seen using a **microscope**. They are called **micro-organisms** or **microbes**. Before the microscope was invented nobody could see microbes.

Microbes include:

● fungi such as moulds and yeast
● tiny one-celled animals (protozoans)
● tiny one-celled plants (plankton)
● bacteria
● viruses.

Microbes are living things. All living **organisms** do the same seven things. You can easily remember them by thinking of 'MRS GREN':

M – movement	G – growth
R – reproduction	R – respiration
S – sensitivity	E – excretion
	N – nutrition (feeding)

Cells

If you look down a microscope you can also see that all plants and animals are made up of lots of tiny units called **cells**.

● Plant leaf cells magnified ×40

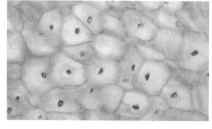

● Human epithelial cells magnified ×100

Chapter 1 looks into the world of cells and microbes. You will learn how the use of technology has enabled scientists to see beyond the limit of the human eye. This has led to important developments in our understanding about life and health.

The information on the CD-ROM might help you decide if something is living.

1 Explain why microscopes are very useful for scientists.
2 Explain why tiny microbes such as bacteria or plankton are living things.

Microscopes

A microscope makes small things look bigger. A typical school light microscope like the one below magnifies between 10 and 400 times. Hospitals and universities have very powerful electron microscopes that can magnify over 100 000 times.

● Using an electron microscope

To find out more about what the parts of the light microscope do, look at the diagram on the CD-ROM.

3 Use a microscope to look at a small drop of pond water. Can you see any microscopic animals moving around? Describe what you see.

4 Use a microscope to look at thin specimens of plant tissue. Your teacher may give you a worksheet to guide you.

5 Write out instructions on how to use a microscope correctly for a person who has never used one before.

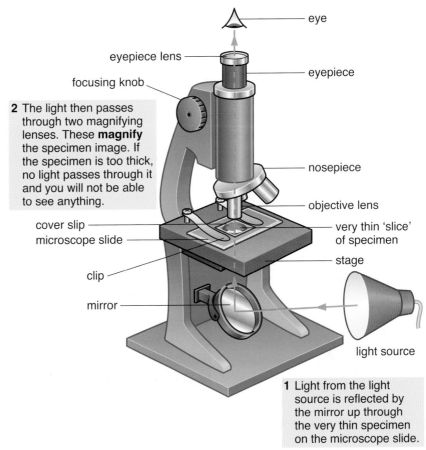

2 The light then passes through two magnifying lenses. These **magnify** the specimen image. If the specimen is too thick, no light passes through it and you will not be able to see anything.

1 Light from the light source is reflected by the mirror up through the very thin specimen on the microscope slide.

● How the light microscope works

This equation is used to work out the **total magnification** of a specimen:

total magnification = magnification of the eyepiece lens × magnification of the objective lens

6 Write down the functions of the following parts of the light microscope. Use the information on the CD-ROM if you need help.

- eyepiece and objective lens
- nosepiece
- lamp
- clips
- stage

Bacteria

The world is full of **bacteria**. We sometimes call harmful bacteria 'germs', but this is not a correct scientific term. Surprisingly, most bacteria in the world are very good for us. They play an essential part in breaking down dead and decaying material and **recycling** the chemicals as useful nutrients for new plant growth.

When bacteria reproduce they just split into two. (You will learn more about this in Chapter 4.) Bacteria can reproduce every 20 minutes in the right conditions – this means they can double their number every 20 minutes!

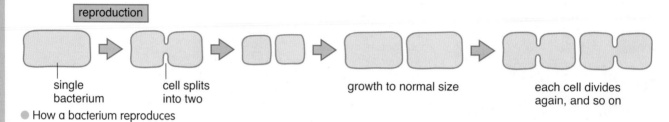

reproduction

single bacterium | cell splits into two | growth to normal size | each cell divides again, and so on

● How a bacterium reproduces

7 Calculate how many bacteria there would be after 24 hours, starting with one reproducing bacterium.

Bacteria will reproduce in any suitable food medium. If they reproduce to a very large number, the clump (**colony**) can eventually be seen. This proves that at least one bacterium was there to start with.

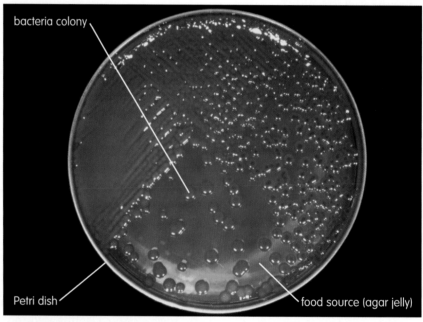

bacteria colony

Petri dish

food source (agar jelly)

● Each colony contains millions of bacteria

Investigating bacteria

You have to be very careful when growing bacteria on Petri dishes. **Microbiologists** work using **sterile** techniques. This means they wear masks and plastic gloves and only handle the bacteria inside special fume cupboards. They **sterilise** all the equipment they need before and after use. This is because any harmful bacteria around might thrive and reproduce. In a school lab you should *never* open a closed Petri dish.

8 Find out if washing your hands removes microbes. Your teacher may give you a worksheet with instructions.

Look on the CD-ROM to find out what qualifications you need to become a microbiologist and to learn more about what microbiologists do.

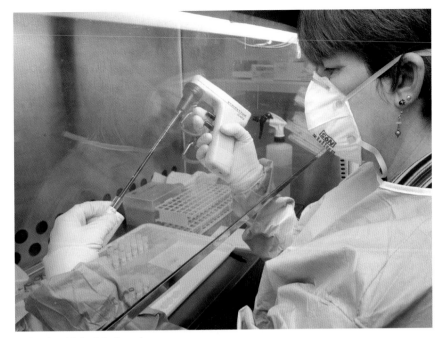

A microbiologist at work

9 A pupil leaves nine sterile agar samples (in Petri dishes) open to the air for 10 minutes. She then closes each dish and keeps them at different temperatures for one day. She then counts the number of colonies of bacteria on each Petri dish. The graph shows the results of her experiment.

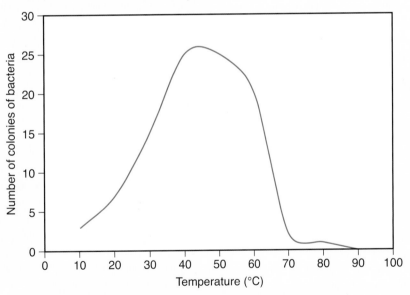

a) At which temperature did the bacteria grow best?

b) If you wanted to prevent the growth of bacteria from the air, at what temperature ranges might you store the sealed Petri dishes?

c) If the Petri dishes were left open to the air for 20 minutes instead of 10 minutes, what difference might you expect in the results?

10 Explain why and how we should work safely when growing bacteria in the school lab.

Useful microbes

Most microbes are very useful to us. Microbes have a bad public image because a few rogue ones cause nasty illnesses.

The bread-making, beer and wine industries

An example of a useful microbe is **yeast**. It is used in the bread-making, beer and wine industries.

Yeast feeds on sugar. As it does so it produces **alcohol** and bubbles of **carbon dioxide**, helping the dough to rise in bread making. The better yeast grows, the more bubbles it produces.

Yeast is a safe microbe to work with in a school lab.

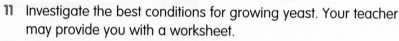

● Yeast is used in the bread-making, beer and wine industries

Read more about yeast on the CD-ROM.

11 Investigate the best conditions for growing yeast. Your teacher may provide you with a worksheet.
12 Why is yeast used in **a)** bread making?
 b) beer and wine making?
13 Sometimes bread is made without yeast (unleavened bread). Follow the web link on the CD-ROM to find out what types of bread are made without yeast and where in the world this is most popular.
14 **a)** Read about the useful microbes in yoghurt on the CD-ROM.
 b) Try making some yoghurt yourself. Your teacher may give you a worksheet.

The role of microbes in food webs

Microbes feed off dead plants and animals and break them down into simple useful minerals again. Microbes are **decomposers** of organic waste within food webs.

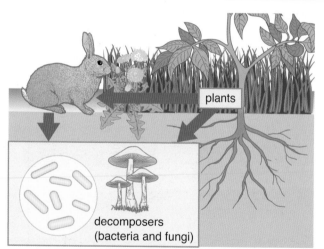

plants

decomposers
(bacteria and fungi)

15 **a)** Identify some decomposers in the food web on the left.
 b) Explain the role of decomposers in food webs.

● Microbes play a vital role in food webs

The role of microbes in recycling

The CD-ROM has a web link where you can find out more on composting.

Read more about how sewage is treated on the CD-ROM.

Recycling of waste is an important world issue. Consider how much waste would be around if there were no microbes.

Everyone can recycle their garden clippings and vegetable waste by using a **composter**, where bacteria and insects eat this waste as their food and recycle the nutrients into the soil for new plant growth.

Where do you think the human waste from toilets goes? It goes to the **sewage** works where bacteria gobble up our waste and recycle it as useful nutrients for fertilising the soil.

Cells, tissues and organs in living things

All living things are made from **cells**. Some microbes are single cells. They are described as **unicellular** organisms.

● Yeast and bacteria are examples of unicellular microbes

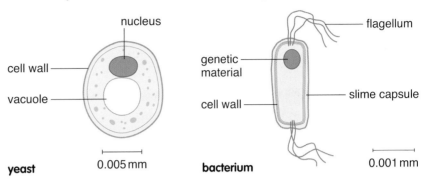

yeast   0.005 mm

bacterium   0.001 mm

Some microbes are made of more than one cell. Larger living things are made of millions of cells. They are called **multicellular** organisms.

Cells are usually grouped together to make **tissues** and **organs** that are normally big enough to see with the naked eye.

A **tissue** is a group of cells with the same size, shape and **function**. Examples of tissues are **muscle** and **nerves**.

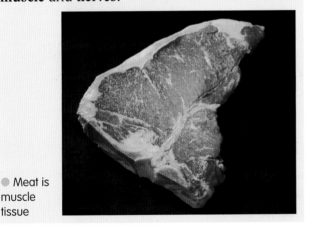

● Meat is muscle tissue

An **organ** is a structure that contains more than one type of tissue. Examples of organs are the **heart** and **brain** in animals and the **leaves** and **roots** in plants.

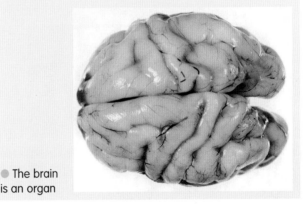

● The brain is an organ

The table below describes the functions of some different tissues.

Tissue	Functions
blood	Carries substances around the body, for example food, oxygen, wastes and hormones
nerve	Transmits impulses from one part of the body to another
muscle	Has lots of long thin cells so that when they all shorten (contract) the muscle can exert enough force to pull on bones
trachea lining	Has cells with little cilia (hair-like structures) which help waft mucus away from the lungs. The mucus catches dust and microbes, so this is a way in which the body protects the lungs from being coated in dust and infections
leaf palisade	Has lots of cells packed with chloroplasts for maximum absorption of light on the top of the leaf
root epidermis	Has hairs which increase the area of the root for maximum water absorption

These diagrams show the main organs in a human and in a plant.

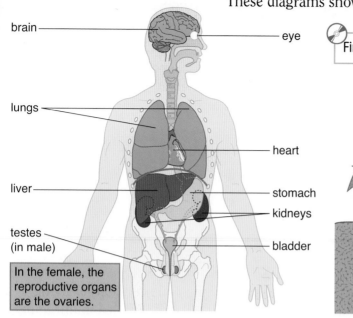

brain — eye

lungs

liver

testes (in male)

heart

stomach

kidneys

bladder

In the female, the reproductive organs are the ovaries.

● Organs in a human

 Find out on the CD-ROM what these organs do.

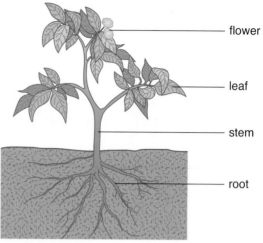

flower

leaf

stem

root

● Organs in a plant

16 Follow the web link to the organ game on the CD-ROM. Play the game.

17 What are the functions of the human and plant organs shown in the diagrams above? (*Hint:* Think what they do in the animal or plant.) Check your answers on the CD-ROM.

18 Explain why a plant is a living thing.

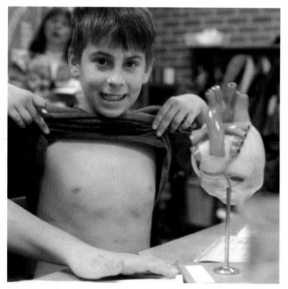

● This young boy would not be alive without his heart transplant

Human organs can sometimes be **transplanted** or donated to save a person's life.

These organs can be transplanted:

- heart
- liver
- lung
- pancreas
- kidney
- cornea (of eye)
- skin (for example in a 'face' transplant)
- bone marrow.

 19 Read the extract 'Living with a liver transplant' on the CD-ROM. Write your own account of what you think a day in the life of a young person with a liver transplant might be like.

Inside cells

Inside all cells there are other structures called **organelles**.

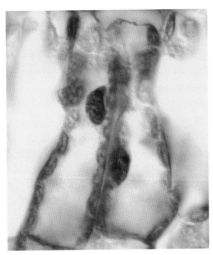

● Plant cells seen with an electron microscope. Can you tell which structures are which using the diagram on the right to help you?

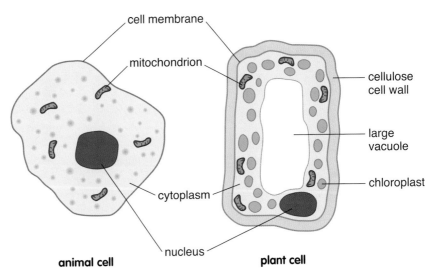

animal cell　　　**plant cell**

The table below shows which organelles are found in plant cells and in animal cells and their functions.

Organelle	Plant	Animal	Functions
nucleus	✔	✔	Controls the cell. Contains DNA
cell membrane	✔	✔	Selectively allows things in and out of the cell
cytoplasm	✔	✔	Jelly-like fluid which contains all the cell's chemicals and organelles between the nucleus and the membrane
mitochondrion	✔	✔	The cell's powerhouse. Provides energy
chloroplast	✔	✗	Green structure that contains chlorophyll, which traps energy from sunlight
cellulose cell wall	✔	✗	Rigid structure that gives strength and shape to cell
large vacuole	✔	✗	Contains cell sap. Keeps cell rigid

20 Explain why plant cells have some organelles that animal cells do not need.
21 Write a paragraph about the differences and similarities between plant and animal cells.
22 Make a model of an animal cell or a plant cell to show the structures.
23 Imagine going on a journey through a huge virtual cell. Write a short story about what you see on your journey.

Different types of cells

Cells come in all shapes and sizes. Their shape and size depend on their function (the job they have to do). The cells are described as **specialised**.

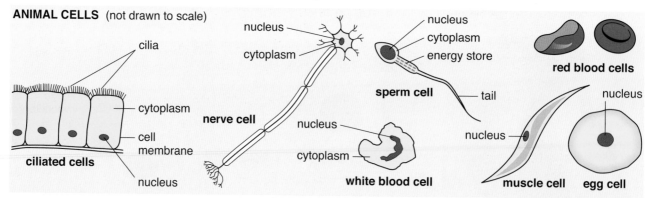

ANIMAL CELLS (not drawn to scale)

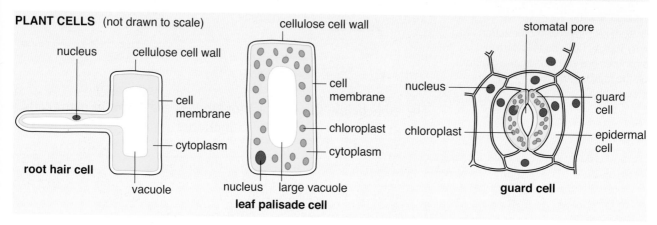

PLANT CELLS (not drawn to scale)

A cell's structure is related to its function. The table below shows some examples.

Read more about the different types of cells on the CD-ROM.

Cell	How structure relates to function
red blood cell	Disc shape maximises surface area to absorb oxygen
nerve cell	Very long thin tubes that can carry messages a long way, for example from the spine to the big toe
sperm cell	Long tail enables it to swim
leaf palisade cell	Contains chloroplasts that use sunlight for photosynthesis

Read the blog on the CD-ROM by a sufferer of leukaemia to learn about the importance of blood cells to our health.

24 Use the diagrams above and the information on the CD-ROM to help you explain how the structures of the following cells are related to their functions:

- muscle cell
- root hair cell
- ciliated cell in the windpipe (trachea)
- egg cell.

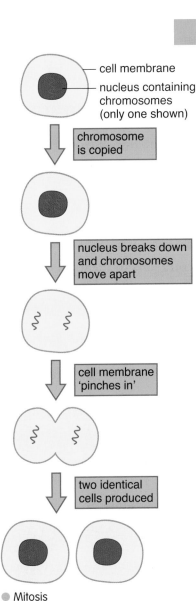

cell membrane

nucleus containing chromosomes (only one shown)

chromosome is copied

nucleus breaks down and chromosomes move apart

cell membrane 'pinches in'

two identical cells produced

● Mitosis

● Cultured tomato plantlets at different stages

Growing cells

Cells are constantly dividing and this causes **growth**. One cell divides into two identical cells. First the nucleus divides into two. The nucleus contains **chromosomes**. New cells usually contain the same chromosomes as the parent cell and so new cells will be identical to the parent cell.

This type of cell division is called **mitosis**. Each new cell grows to full size before it divides again.

25 Follow the web link on the CD-ROM to the animation of mitosis. Play the animation, then explain how cell division causes growth.

The cells in our bodies do not last for ever – they age and die. Some cells, for example those that line the gut, skin and blood cells, have a very fast 'turnover'. This means that new cells are made constantly, even during adulthood.

Stem cells are very important. They are immature cells that can keep on multiplying whenever needed and can **differentiate** into specialised cells after cell division. This happens in the body when cells die and need to be replaced.

Did you know that most household dust is dead skin cells that are constantly worn away from the surface of our bodies?

26 Explain how the body repairs itself after injury.
27 Look on the CD-ROM to find out which cells need replacing all the time.
28 Look on the CD-ROM to find out how stem cells can be used in medicine.

Scientists use stem cells from humans in **tissue culture** for medical research and to grow healthy tissue. For example, patients with leukaemia can have healthy stem cells transplanted into their bone marrow to replace diseased cells that are killed by radiotherapy treatment.

29 Why must tissue culture be kept sterile?

Tissue culture is very useful in horticulture to grow crops – for example, carrots can be grown from just a few cells.

How the microscope helped scientific and medical discovery

Before the microscope was invented no one knew about microscopic structures such as cells or microbes, for example bacteria and viruses.

Lenses had been used in Asia to magnify things from 1000 AD. Spectacles, telescopes and microscopes were developed from lenses and by 1600 were in common use around Europe. The development of microscopes went as follows.

- The first **light microscopes** were made in Holland in the 16th century. They had just one lens.
- In 1665 Robert Hooke added a second lens to make an object look even bigger. This was called a **compound microscope**. He first saw tiny compartments in tissue from thin pieces of cork plant. He called these compartment 'cells'.
- In 1674, after many improvements in the design of microscopes, Antonie van Leeuwenhoek was the first person to see microbes.
- In 1931 Ernst Ruska invented the **electron microscope**, which uses electrons instead of light. Very fine detail of cells, bacteria and viruses could be seen for the first time.

Medical and health discoveries associated with microscope use are as follows.

- In the 17th, 18th and 19th centuries, scientists used microscopes to explore where microbes were found. They found them everywhere – in the air, in water, in food, milk and wine, on people's bodies, and in people's wounds, boils, teeth and breath!
- Scientists began to get evidence that many diseases were spread by microbes. In 1854 John Snow identified microbes in drinking water as the source of a cholera outbreak in London. In 1875, Robert Koch proved that anthrax (a disease in sheep) was caused by microbes.

Because of these and other discoveries, public health and hygiene improved dramatically and fewer people died from infectious diseases.

● Hand lenses are still in use today

Find out more about the history of the different types of microscopes on the CD-ROM.

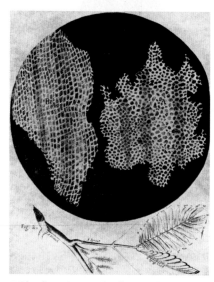

● The first picture of cells in cork tissue seen with a microscope was published by Robert Hooke in his book *Micrographia*

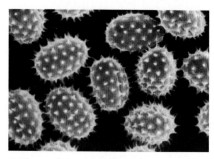

● The surfaces of pollen grains seen using an electron microscope

30 Using the information on this page and on the CD-ROM, draw a timeline linking the development of microscopes with knowledge of how diseases are spread.

31 Write a short story imagining you are an early scientist using a simple microscope and making new discoveries.

32 Read about careers in electron microscopy on the CD-ROM and write about 'A day in the life of an electron microscopist'.

What are viruses?

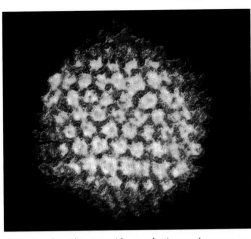

● A virus head seen with an electron microscope

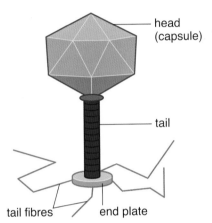

head (capsule)

tail

tail fibres   end plate

● Diagram of a typical virus structure

Viruses are so tiny that you need an electron microscope to see them. A virus next to a flea is roughly equivalent to a human next to a mountain twice the size of Mount Everest! The majority of viruses that have been studied have a diameter between 10 and 300 **nanometres** (1 nanometre = 0.000000001 m). Viruses have interesting shapes rather like crystals.

Viruses need other cells in order to reproduce. They are **parasites** – they live off other living things and do not contribute anything positive in return. They can cause some nasty diseases.

The virus 'cell' does not contain a proper nucleus or any of the other normal organelles. It is a shell around some DNA which is its genetic material. In fact many scientists do not consider a virus to be a true living thing as it cannot exist on its own.

To reproduce, a virus enters into a living **host** cell and releases its DNA into the cell. The virus then takes over the host cell's organelles and chemicals to reproduce its own DNA and make new viruses. This is shown below.

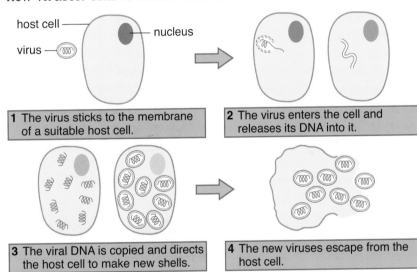

1 The virus sticks to the membrane of a suitable host cell.

2 The virus enters the cell and releases its DNA into it.

3 The viral DNA is copied and directs the host cell to make new shells.

4 The new viruses escape from the host cell.

33 Use the series of diagrams on the right to explain in a letter to a friend how a virus infects another cell.

34 List the diseases that are caused by viruses. Which viral diseases still cannot be prevented by vaccinations?

35 Find the information on the CD-ROM about whether viruses are living things or not. Write down the evidence for and against the idea that viruses are *not* really living things.

Look on the CD-ROM to find out names of common diseases caused by bacteria.

Antibiotic medicines can kill bacteria but do not usually kill viruses. **Viral diseases** such as the common cold, flu, measles, mumps, rubella and chicken pox need to be prevented by **vaccination.**

Usually doctors do not vaccinate people against mild diseases such as colds or mild forms of flu because there are so many different strains of the viruses and it is better for people to build their own immunity. Research on vaccinations against some viral diseases such as HIV/AIDS is ongoing. Some nasty viral diseases such as smallpox and polio have been virtually eliminated as a result of world vaccination programmes.

I hope you like it. It's made from wool. Totally natural. It has no chemicals in it at all.

1 Do you agree with the girl's granny in the cartoon above? Explain your answer.

What is everything made from?

Some substances are manmade. We know that different chemicals have been used to make them. Other substances are found in nature. We say they are natural.

But everything must be made of something. The question is 'what?'

For thousands of years people wondered about what everything is made from. They came up with ideas based on everyday things that they saw in nature. In Ancient Greece some great thinkers (philosophers) thought they had the answer. The Ancient Greek philosopher Thales thought that everything was made from water.

● Thales noticed shells in some pieces of rock

● Thales saw water bubbling out of the ground

2 Look at these cartoons of Thales. Explain how these observations of nature may have led Thales to believe that everything was made from water.

Later another Greek philosopher called Empedocles proposed that everything was made out of four elements – *earth*, *air*, *fire* and *water*. We now know that this is not true, but it was still believed as late as the 1500s.

3 Print out the cartoon of Empedocles from the CD-ROM and complete the thought bubbles to explain how he came up with his ideas.

The elements

We now know that all materials are made out of around 100 pure **elements**. The elements look very different from each other and have a wide variety of different **properties**. Each element has its own **symbol**. This is a short way of writing its name, just as we can use our initials instead of our name.

Most elements have symbols based on one or two letters from their name. For example the symbol for aluminium is Al. There are often lots of elements starting with the same letter. The second letter in the symbol is not always the second letter in the element's name. For example there are 11 elements starting with the letter C.

A few elements have symbols that have totally different letters from those in their names. This is because the symbol is based on the Latin name for the element. For example the symbol for gold is Au; the Latin for gold is *aurum*.

We use a lot of different elements in everyday life. Each element has characteristic properties. When an object is designed, the element that has the right properties to make it do its job properly is chosen. This could mean choosing the element that looks best, or one that does not melt even at a very high temperature, or one for which each 1 cm3 of the element has a very low mass.

Look on the CD-ROM to see these 11 'C' elements listed.

4 What is the symbol for caesium? Using the information on the CD-ROM, explain why caesium has this symbol.

Look on the CD-ROM for more elements that have symbols based on their Latin names.

5 a) Find out how each of these elements is used in everyday life: chlorine (Cl), copper (Cu), helium (He), iron (Fe), magnesium (Mg), mercury (Hg), neon (Ne), silver (Ag). Give one example of each.
   b) What property makes each of them suited to this purpose?

6 Print out the pictures on the CD-ROM. Label each picture with the name of the element being used and the main property of the element that makes it a good choice.

● Aluminium (Al) is a fairly light element and it is used to make drinks cans

● Gold (Au) is used to make jewellery because it is shiny and has an attractive colour

Some elements are not in everyday use because they are **hazardous**. They may be toxic, or give off toxic fumes, or they may be highly flammable. Scientists know how to use them safely and are therefore able to use them in investigations. Sometimes scientists need special equipment to keep them safe when they are handling these elements.

7 Suggest what precautions scientists take to enable them to work safely with hazardous elements.

Trying to make gold

For many centuries alchemists worked on one problem – 'How do you turn a base (ordinary) metal into gold?' We now know that this task was scientifically impossible. An element *can* be made by reacting chemicals together, as long as one of the chemicals in the reaction already contains the element. The alchemists could never have succeeded because they were using base metals, which were elements. These did not contain any gold, because elements cannot be broken down into any other simpler substance.

But by trying to make their fortune the alchemists did manage to discover many other, useful things.

Use this print of an alchemist at work with his assistants to answer the questions.

There is an interactive version of the picture on the CD-ROM, which you can enlarge.

8　Can you find these things in the picture?

　　　a tripod, tongs, a flask, a balance, a timer

9　How are substances being heated in the picture?

10　What other pieces of apparatus can you see?

● The Alchemist engraved by Hieronymous Cock, after a painting by Pieter Brueghel, c.1558

Alchemists worked and experimented all over the world. Often they made discoveries independently of one another. Their only form of communication was through the written word.

11　Look at the table of alchemists' names on the CD-ROM. Research using web sites the dates when they lived, where they worked and what their key discoveries were. Fill in the table using the information you have found.

12　Write a letter to an alchemist. Try to persuade the alchemist using a chemical argument that he is wasting his time trying to change other metals into gold.
　　Use the letter outline on the CD-ROM if you need help.

13　Find out about and describe one key discovery of one of the alchemists that is still being used today.

Controlling fire

The alchemists needed to heat the elements (and other chemicals) to change them. Sometimes they wanted to melt or boil them to make them into a liquid or gas. On other occasions they heated them to make them burn in the air. This allowed them to make new chemicals. The alchemists simply made a small fire, but today this would not be regarded as safe. A fire is also very difficult to adjust, making experiments difficult to control properly. Modern chemists need a way to heat and burn things that is controlled and safe!

14 For each way of heating shown in the pictures, list the advantages and disadvantages of the method for experiments in the lab.

● There are many ways of using fire to heat things

15 Print out the cartoon of Year 7 pupils carrying out an experiment from the CD-ROM. Circle anything you see that is incorrect or unsafe (there are ten things to spot).

16 a) Find five different items used for heating at home (for example a hair dryer). Ask the owner/user of each item to explain how they use it safely.

   b) Complete the report form from the CD-ROM. You could include a photo of each person with their heating equipment on the form.

The Bunsen burner

The **Bunsen burner** was invented in the 19th century. It is named after the scientist Robert Bunsen.

The Bunsen burner flame can be carefully controlled, using the air hole. It is much safer than an open fire but it must still be used correctly.

17 Look on the CD-ROM to learn more about the development of the Bunsen burner. Do you think we should call the Bunsen burner by this name, or should it be named after someone else?

18 Imagine that Robert Bunsen is applying for a scientific job. Find the application form on the CD-ROM and fill in his application. (*Remember:* he is trying to make himself look as good as possible!)

● Bunsen burners are usually used with other lab apparatus

Sorting the elements

Solid, liquid or gas?

We can work out whether an element is a **solid**, a **liquid** or a **gas** (at room temperature) by using information about its melting and boiling points. Room temperature is always taken to be 25 °C.

- The **melting point** is the temperature at which an element changes on heating from a solid into a liquid.
- The **boiling point** is the temperature at which an element changes on heating from a liquid into a gas.

Element	Melting point (°C)	Boiling point (°C)
caesium	28.7	690
bromine	−7.2	58.8
chlorine	−101	−34.7
fluorine	−220	−188
mercury	−38.9	357
iodine	114	184

19 Use the interactive thermometer on the CD-ROM to work out whether caesium, bromine and chlorine are solids, liquids or gases at room temperature.

20 Look at the data for fluorine, mercury and iodine in the table above. At room temperature, which of these elements will be a solid, which a liquid and which a gas?

Metal or non-metal?

Metals and **non-metals** have very distinctive properties.

Properties of a metal	Properties of a typical non-metal
High melting point	Low melting point
Dense	Brittle (if solid)
Shiny	Dull
Good conductor of electricity	Poor conductor of electricity
Good conductor of heat	Poor conductor of heat
Malleable (can be hammered into shape)	
Ductile (can be drawn into wires)	
Sonorous (rings when struck)	

21 Print out a copy of the cartoon on the CD-ROM. On your printout circle where metals are being used and add a label for each use to say which property (or properties) of the metal is (are) important.

A chemical jigsaw

It took many years for scientists to be able to fully organise all the known elements in a useful way. Look at the cartoons below.

"Lithium, sodium and potassium are all similar. They make a triad."

● Döbereiner noticed that there were groups of three similar elements. He called the groups 'triads'

"The elements are just like eight-note octaves on the piano. When I arrange them in order of their atomic weight, the eighth element is similar to the first one."

● Newlands arranged the elements in order of atomic weight. There seemed to be a pattern that similar elements were found every eight elements – but it didn't always work

"The elements definitely make groups. I'm sure atomic weight has something to do with it, but what?"

"I can't get these cards to fit the pattern... Ah, I know what I can try!"

"Those elements are the wrong way round – their atomic weights must be wrong! And there's a gap there – there must be an element yet to be discovered!"

● Mendeleev made cards with the elements' names and atomic weights on. He tried to arrange them in order of atomic weight but realised that some needed to be swapped, and he made the creative leap of allowing gaps for elements that had not yet been discovered

You can see Mendeleev's original table on the CD-ROM.

Dmitri Mendeleev was a Russian chemist in the 19th century who came up with an idea and stuck with it. He had noticed repeating patterns in the elements and called his organisation of elements the **Periodic Table**. Where his pattern broke down he claimed that it was because some elements were missing. He thought it was because they had still to be discovered.

Mendeleev successfully predicted the properties of several missing elements. This helped his idea to be accepted. The Periodic Table has been improved over the years but it is still based on Mendeleev's original design.

You can find the modern Periodic Table on the CD-ROM.

22 One of the gaps that Mendeleev left in his table was for an element between silicon and tin in one of the vertical columns. Read the information about silicon and tin on the CD-ROM. Then write a short description of what you think the missing element might be like.

23 Look up the name of the missing element on the modern Periodic Table. Find out what it is like. Were your predictions correct?

24 Use a flow diagram to summarise how scientists gradually developed the Periodic Table.

How small?

Imagine that you could break up a sample of an element into smaller and smaller pieces. The smallest part that an element could theoretically be divided into is called an **atom**. An individual atom is so small that it cannot be seen even using a light microscope or an electron microscope (see page 7). Understanding the arrangement and movement of atoms helps us to explain the properties of elements. For example it can help us to predict how elements behave as a solid, liquid or gas.

Because atoms cannot be seen, it can be tricky to think about and understand them. Sometimes scientists use models and diagrams to help. These may not be exactly the same as the 'real thing' but it is much easier to have a picture in your head.

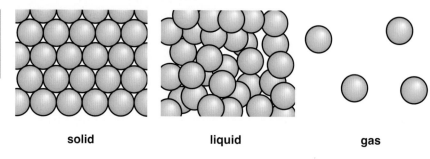

solid　　　　**liquid**　　　　**gas**

● The arrangement of atoms in a solid, a liquid and a gas

If a model still does not help, scientists may come up with an **analogy** to help explain something. An analogy relates the thing that is proving difficult to think about (in our case the arrangement of atoms in an element) to something we experience every day (for example the movement of pupils around a school).

25 Look at the pictures of some very small objects on the CD-ROM. List these objects in order of size (from smallest to biggest).

Look on the CD-ROM to see animated versions of these diagrams.

26 Look at the pictures on the right. Describe how each pair of pictures shows analogies of a solid and a gas. Which pair do you think is better and why?

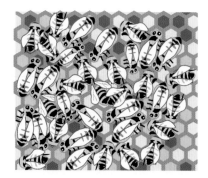

27 Make up your own analogy that works well for a solid and a gas. You might be able to use clipart to create your analogies.

It is now possible to create images of atoms. The image below was produced using a scanning tunnelling microscope. This microscope uses electrical signals that can then be processed to create a picture. The image shows iron atoms on the surface of copper metal.

● We can now create images of atoms using incredibly powerful microscopes – the iron atoms are shown in blue

● A mercury thermometer – thermometers like this have mainly been replaced with safer alternatives

28 Look in books or follow the web link on the CD-ROM to find out how a scanning tunnelling microscope works. Produce a labelled diagram or a 3D model to explain very simply how the microscope works. (Even university students would find a detailed explanation hard, so only the basics are needed!)

There are lots of liquids in everyday life but liquid *elements* are very unusual. Mercury is a liquid metal and was known to the Ancient Greeks, Romans, Chinese and Hindus. Its symbol, Hg, comes from the Latin *hydrargyrum* meaning 'liquid silver'. In fact it used to be called quicksilver.

Mercury is still used in some thermometers to measure temperature although safer alternatives have largely replaced them.

29 Draw a diagram to show the arrangement of atoms in mercury. Either use your own analogy from question 27 or one of the two analogies used in question 26 to create an analogy for the arrangement and movement of atoms in a liquid.

30 Use the melting point and boiling point data on the CD-ROM to find three other metals that are not liquids at standard room temperature but that would be liquids on a hot (30 °C) summer's day.

Chlorine: good or bad?

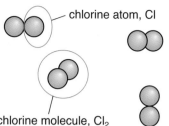
chlorine atom, Cl

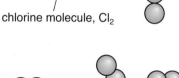
chlorine molecule, Cl₂

The element chlorine is a gas that can do both a lot of harm and a lot of good. Like many other gases its atoms actually join together in pairs. We call these pairs of atoms **molecules**. The chemical formula for a chlorine molecule is Cl_2.

In the First World War chlorine gas was used as a weapon to kill enemy soldiers. The effects were devastating.

In many countries people die of diseases that would be preventable if only they had clean drinking water. Water can be purified by using chlorine, as shown in the photos below.

● Chlorine gas

● Is chlorine good or bad?

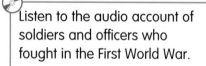
Listen to the audio account of soldiers and officers who fought in the First World War.

31 Write an essay outlining the good and bad that chlorine can do. Conclude your essay with a paragraph explaining whether you think chlorine is good or bad.
Use the pictures on the CD-ROM to help you to write each paragraph of your essay.

32 Nowadays the use of chemical weapons is illegal under international law. Find out what has been agreed under the Hague Convention and the Geneva Protocol.

33 When a natural disaster strikes, one of the biggest dangers, after the disaster itself, is the risk of disease. Find out which diseases can be spread by water and what steps aid agencies take to prevent the spread of such diseases. How does the Unicef Family Survival Kit listed below help?

Unicef Family Survival Kit:
Cooking utensils, Blankets, Clothing, Oral rehydration salts to fight diarrhoea, Chlorine tablets to purify water, Soaps, Bucket and other hygiene items, Candles and kerosene lanterns

3 Big ideas

◼ Physics questions

How big is the Universe?

How many X-rays can you have before you glow in the dark?

Why is the sky blue?

What is the smallest particle?

Where does the electricity come from?

How can you walk on custard?

Is a spider's web stronger than steel?

Can I make a dress from optical fibres?

There are so many questions that scientists try to answer. However, often when one question is answered many other questions pop up! Scientists also try to produce evidence from experiments to back up their answers. So science involves a lot of creative thoughts and ideas, and lots of experimenting. As time goes by, evidence builds up to support particular ideas – so much so that the ideas become 'accepted'. But, in actual fact, there is always the possibility that an experiment will come along to disprove ideas that have been around a long time. For example from the days of Newton in the 17th century to the present day there have been many arguments about the true nature of light.

Philosophy is all about thoughts and ideas. Physicists used to be called natural philosophers. In other words they were people who asked questions about the natural world, and came up with ideas to help answer these questions and practical ideas to give evidence for these answers.

This chapter gives an overview of some of the big ideas that physicists are interested in.

On the CD-ROM you will find a web link to a conversation with an astronaut and a video of life in a space station and space walks.

You can read about the Big Bang theory on the CD-ROM. There is also a web link for you to follow.

You can find out about light years and big numbers on the CD-ROM.

All that Space

The **Universe** contains all the matter and energy in existence. The best theory about how the Universe began is the Big Bang theory. We think that the Big Bang occurred about 15 billion years ago.

Immediately after the Big Bang the Universe started expanding and the furthest galaxies detected at present are about 13 billion light years away (130 billion trillion kilometres).

● This is a picture of galaxies in deep Space taken by the Hubble Space Telescope

All the dots in this picture are galaxies but they occupy only a very small part of the Universe. There are billions and billions of galaxies in the Universe. The Universe is almost all empty space with just some objects in it.

● Here are some objects you might encounter if you could travel through the Universe. These have been photographed using telescopes

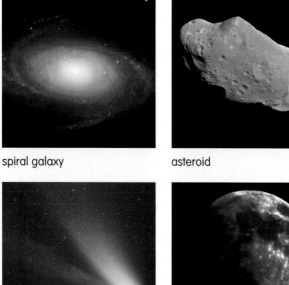
spiral galaxy

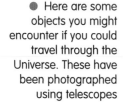
asteroid

bright star

comet

Moon

Saturn

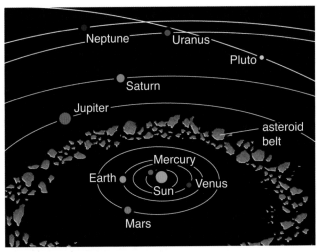

● Our Solar System

Find out more about objects in the Solar System on the CD-ROM.

Where in the Universe do we live?

We live on the planet Earth, which is part of our **Solar System**.

The Solar System is a collection of **planets**, **asteroids** and **comets** all orbiting the **Sun**, **moons** that orbit the planets, and **meteors**.

So, our Space address is:

Earth
3rd planet from the Sun
Solar System
Milky Way
Universe

1 Look at the pictures of the galaxy, asteroid, star, comet, Moon and Saturn at the bottom of page 28. Some of these objects exist in our Solar System and some further away in Space. Put them in order of size.

2 Most of the objects in the pictures can be seen with the naked eye. What are the advantages of using the following and what further details can be seen using each of them?

- A telescope.
- The Hubble Space Telescope.

3 a) Use the web link on the CD-ROM to research the different features of the planets of the Solar System. Summarise the properties of the planets in a table like this:

Size compared with Earth	Rocky or gas?	How hot or cold?	Atmosphere composed of

b) Decide which planet you would most like to visit. Write a travel article saying roughly how long it would take to get there and what you are looking forward to seeing and experiencing when you arrive.

4 The Andromeda Galaxy is our galactic neighbour. It is only 2.2 million light years away. Write instructions to an intergalactic courier so that she can deliver a letter from your penfriend in the Andromeda Galaxy to your house. Is there anything that she should avoid on the way?

As time goes by

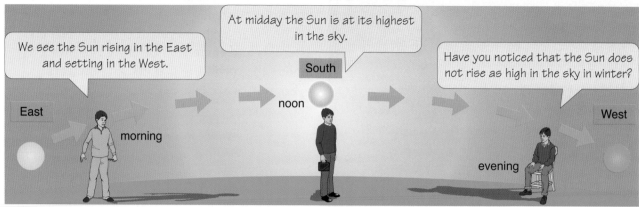

We see the Sun rising in the East and setting in the West.

At midday the Sun is at its highest in the sky.

Have you noticed that the Sun does not rise as high in the sky in winter?

East

morning

South

noon

West

evening

● The Sun moves through the sky during the day, from sunrise to sunset

● A **day** is the time it takes the Earth to spin once on its axis.
● A **month** is the time it takes the Moon to go once around the Earth.
● A **year** is the time it takes the Earth to go once around the Sun.

Follow the web link on the CD-ROM to find instructions on how to make a sundial.

The Sun has been a key factor in deciding the definition of days and years in most cultures. Sundials have been used since the first cave-dwellers started noticing how the length and position of shadows varied during the day and how the height of the Sun varied at different times of the year.

Jasmine read that the Sun lit up different amounts of the Moon through the month. She decided to draw the Moon in her diary each night for one month. Here are some of her pictures.

Look on the CD-ROM to see how the changing positions of the Sun, the Earth and the Moon cause these changing shapes.

4 February
I can't see the Moon

11 February
I can see a Half Moon

18 February
I can see a Full Moon

5 Explain how the Sun's rays light up none, half or all of the Moon to give the shapes recorded in Jasmine's diary.

Orreries

The path of an object around another object is called its **orbit**.

An orrery is a model of the Solar System used to show the positions and motions of the planets orbiting a stationary Sun. It can be used to find relative year lengths and to predict eclipses. Sometimes orreries were driven by a motor. The first modern Sun-centred orrery was made by George Graham in the 18th century.

● This picture of children looking at an orrery was painted in 1766 by Joseph Wright. They were using a lamp as the Sun

On the CD-ROM there is an activity that helps to explain the seasons.

Seasons

The **seasons** are directly related to the angle at which the Sun's rays reach the Earth.

- In summer the Sun is more directly overhead and its rays travel through less atmosphere. They are more intense and the weather is warmer.
- In winter the Sun is lower and the Sun's rays do not reach the Earth at such a direct angle. The rays travel through more atmosphere and are less intense. The weather is colder.

● The four seasons

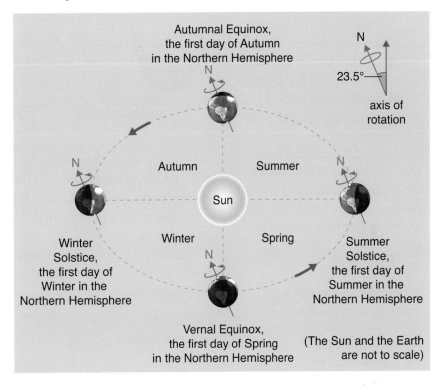

Autumnal Equinox, the first day of Autumn in the Northern Hemisphere

23.5°

axis of rotation

Autumn   Summer

Sun

Winter   Spring

Winter Solstice, the first day of Winter in the Northern Hemisphere

Summer Solstice, the first day of Summer in the Northern Hemisphere

Vernal Equinox, the first day of Spring in the Northern Hemisphere

(The Sun and the Earth are not to scale)

Look on the CD-ROM for pictures of some of these structures.

We have calendars on our walls, on our computers and on our mobile phones. Ancient people of many cultures built structures such as Stonehenge to identify important dates.

6 Imagine that you were living in the Stone Age. What regular features in the day and night sky would you notice as time passed?

7 It takes about 29 Earth years for Saturn to orbit the Sun. But it takes Saturn only 11 hours to spin once on its axis.
   a) How many Saturn days are there in an Earth day?
   b) If you are 11 years old on Earth, how old will you be on Saturn?

8 Explain why the Sun is higher in the sky and it is hotter in summer than in winter.

9 The circumference of the Earth at the equator is about 40 000 km. Work out approximately how fast the people living at the equator are travelling as the Earth spins on its axis once every 24 hours. (*Note:* You will be surprised how fast it is – and we do not even feel it!)

Force effects – getting things done

Forces get things done. The pictures show the sorts of things that forces can do.

● Forces make things happen

speed up   slow down   stop

start   change shape   change direction

10 Read the extract by Michael Owen on the CD-ROM, paying special attention to the underlined phrases. Write a paragraph explaining how a knowledge of the physics of forces would help improve your football skills.

Look on the CD-ROM to learn more about Hooke and Newton.

11 Why is force measured in newtons?

12 a) What is the value of each force in the pictures?

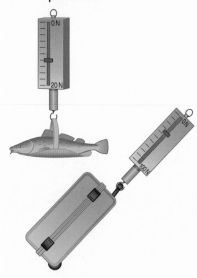

b) Explain how a newtonmeter works.

How do we know how big a force is? A common way to find out is to use a **newtonmeter**. In 1660 Robert Hooke found that springs extend by the same amount when the force on them is increased by equal amounts. A newtonmeter is made of a spring with a hook.

The unit for force is the **newton**. This unit is named after Isaac Newton. Hooke and Newton were great rivals.

Forces usually act in pairs.

● When you are standing still, your **weight** is acting downwards and the reaction of the ground is acting upwards. These forces are equal and opposite.

● If you are running along, your **forward thrust** will be pushing you forward and **air resistance** and **friction** will be tending to slow you down. When you start off your forward thrust will be bigger than the air resistance and you will get faster (**accelerate**).

● When you slow down, the air resistance will be bigger than the forward thrust.

13 Make matchstick men sketches of the pictures of the boy above. Draw arrows on your diagrams to show the pairs of forces. Show where each force is acting and in what direction. Indicate the relative sizes of the forces by altering the length of the arrows.

Hidden forces

Forces at a distance

Some forces do not need to be in contact with an object to affect it. **Gravity**, **magnetic** forces and **electrostatic** forces all behave like this.

Gravity is pulling the skydiver towards the Earth.

The steel object is held in mid-air by a magnetic force.

The electrostatic force is pulling the cat's hair upwards.

14 a) Draw a picture of the Earth going around the Sun. Draw on it the direction of the force of gravity on the Earth. What object is causing this force?

   b) The bigger the object, the bigger the force of gravity around it and the further it reaches. Explain why the Sun has eight planets orbiting it but the Earth has only one small moon.

Force fields

Physicists call the area over which these non-contact forces act a **field**. A magnetic field is the area around a magnet in which a magnetic material will be pulled towards the magnet. We can see magnetic field patterns using iron filings.

● A magnetic field is invisible but we can see it by using iron filings which line up along the magnetic field lines

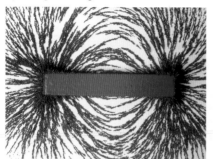

single bar magnet

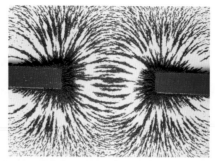

two attracting bar magnets

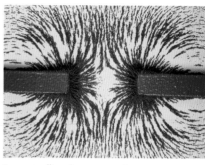

two repelling bar magnets

Did you know that the Earth behaves like a giant magnet?

Read more about magnetic materials and the Earth's own magnetic field on the CD-ROM.

Follow the web link on the CD-ROM to calculate what your weight would be on different planets.

15 Iron, nickel and cobalt are the only elements that are attracted by a magnet. Explain how drinks cans can be sorted for recycling using a magnet. Look on the CD-ROM for help with this question and follow the web link to learn more.

As well as a magnetic field, the Earth has a gravitational field all around it. In this gravitational field objects are pulled towards the Earth. For example, apples fall off trees to the ground.

Weight is the force of gravity on an object. The weight of anything will vary on different planets but the mass stays the same. On Earth:

weight (in newtons) = mass (in kg) $\times$ 10

Friction

Friction is a force that acts between two touching surfaces. It is always there but because we cannot see it we tend to forget about it. But it stops your feet slipping when you stand up – unless you are on ice where the friction force is very small!

16 Write an advertisement for a climbing shoe using the idea of friction. Say why it is important for there to be lots of friction between the shoe and the rocks. You can use the web link on the CD-ROM to give you some ideas.

Charge!

Why does the television screen get so dusty?

Why do I sometimes get a shock from the car door?

Why does an aeroplane have metal strips in its tyres?

Why do I hear crackles when I take off a jumper?

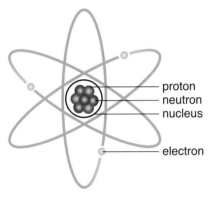

proton
neutron
nucleus

electron

● An atom's structure

Look at the animation of this on the CD-ROM.

We make use of static electricity for many things including cling film, photocopying, painting road signs and fridges, and cleaning the discharges from factory chimneys. Look on the CD-ROM to see how these things work.

Look on the CD-ROM to learn more about the risks of static electricity.

An **electrostatic** force causes things to be either **attracted** or **repelled**. It acts between electric **charges**. There are two types of charge. We call these **positive** and **negative** charges.

Where do these charges come from? There is no charge on an **atom** – we say that it is **neutral**. In the middle of the atom is a nucleus made up of positively charged and neutral particles. These are called protons and neutrons. Around this nucleus there are negatively charged particles called **electrons**, which orbit it. (It is a bit like a microscopic Solar System.)

Electrons are very small compared to protons and neutrons and can be moved away from the atom. If some negatively charged electrons get away from the atom we are left with a positive particle and free electrons. These charged particles can now exert a force on each other, and things will move.

You can charge a balloon by rubbing it on your jumper. Electrons will be rubbed on to the balloon and it will have negative charge. It will then attract your hair or a thin stream of water from the tap.

There is an electrostatic rule:

Like charges repel; unlike charges attract.

The charges that build up on objects can cause sparks or shocks, so we need to be careful.

17 Can you answer the questions at the top of the page? Look on the CD-ROM for help if you need it.

18 a) Look at the diagram of the Van de Graaff generator on CD-ROM. How is the charge produced? Where is the charge stored? If you need help, you can reveal the answers on-screen.

b) Explain why there is a spark when a metal sphere is brought close to a charged Van de Graaff generator.

Making the charges move

In 1752 Benjamin Franklin showed, by his now famous experiment, that lightning is a form of electricity.

Find out more on the CD-ROM.

19 What was the naturally occurring source of static electricity that Benjamin Franklin used?

● Franklin's lightning experiment

Read on the CD-ROM about Volta, Henry and others who experimented with electric circuits and invented various electrical devices.

Franklin's experiment started the thought in other scientists' minds that electricity may be able to flow if it is given a pathway to flow along.

Although static electricity has some interesting and useful effects, electricity became really useful when Alessandro Volta invented the battery and when Joseph Henry connected a wire to a battery and sent an electric current through a copper wire.

An electric **current** occurs when there is a flow of charge through a conductor such as a wire.

The parallel plate experiment

The diagram below shows an experiment with a Van de Graaff generator and conducting parallel plates.

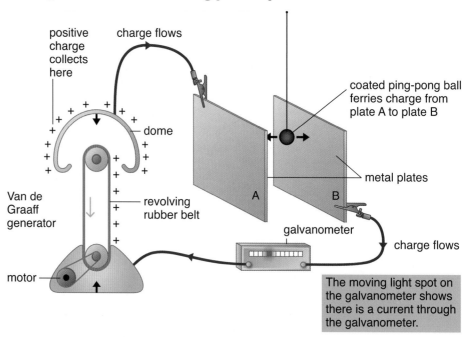

positive charge collects here

charge flows

coated ping-pong ball ferries charge from plate A to plate B

dome

metal plates

Van de Graaff generator

revolving rubber belt

A

B

galvanometer

motor

charge flows

The moving light spot on the galvanometer shows there is a current through the galvanometer.

The experiment shows that an electric current is a flow of electrical charge. When the Van de Graaff generator is started the light spot on the galvanometer moves.

What is happening? The belt on the Van de Graaff generator collects positive charge by friction as it moves. The charge is transferred upwards and stored on the dome.

The wire provides a pathway for the charge to flow from the sphere to plate A. The ping-pong ball with a conducting coating picks up charge from plate A and transfers it to plate B. The wire then provides a pathway for the charge from plate B, through the galvanometer and back to the Van de Graaff generator.

Follow the web links on the CD-ROM to help you make circuits work.

You need a closed loop for there to be a path for the charge to flow around. This closed loop is called a **circuit**.

The size of the electric current depends on how much charge is flowing per second.

20 What sort of material can electric charges move along?

Use the information on the CD-ROM to help you answer the next questions.

21 Make a timeline from 1700 to 1900. Label and illustrate your timeline with the major scientists and their experiments in the development of electricity.

22 a) Name four different devices that were the direct outcomes of finding that electricity can flow through wires.

b) What are the two means of early communications mentioned, and who helped develop them?

Fruity electricity

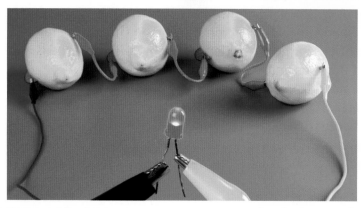

● Lemon electricity!

Look at the animated lemon circuit on the CD-ROM.

The first battery was made in 1798 by the Italian physicist Alessandro Volta. He used copper and zinc discs in an acid solution.

The LED in the picture will only light if there is a power supply and a pathway for the electric charges to flow along. In this case the charges (electrons) are already in the wires. The lemons with the metal electrodes (coins and nails) provide the energy to make them move through the **circuit.**

Electricity is a very useful form of energy because it can be transferred into many other forms of energy using everyday devices such as light bulbs, radios, electric heaters and electric drills.

23 Copy and complete the table to sort the following into different parts of an electric circuit.

lemon, wire, battery, ammeter, light bulb, solar cell, metal strip, motor, television, dynamo, LED, hair dryer

Provider of electrical energy	Pathway for charge to flow	Device that uses electrical energy

Most electrical devices that we use at home are connected by electric plugs in the house to the National Grid. Power stations provide the electricity for the National Grid and most of these use fossil fuels or nuclear energy.

However there are other sources of electricity that we use.

● Solar cells

● Dynamo

● Batteries

On the CD-ROM you can learn about the three sources of electricity shown above.

24 List the advantages and disadvantages of the three sources of electrical energy shown above.
25 Write a leaflet to help homeowners understand how solar panels and dynamos work. Include in your leaflet how they could be used in people's houses and what the advantages are.
 Look at the information on the CD-ROM if you need help.

Energy makes the world go round

To run, skateboard or cycle we need **energy**. We get our energy from food. But where does the energy stored in the food originate? It comes from the Sun. A food chain shows the energy flows.

 energy   energy   energy

● Energy comes from the Sun and is stored in food chains

You will learn more about food chains in Chapter 7.

Fuel and energy

Fuels are sources of energy that can be used to get jobs done. To release this energy most fuels need to go through a **chemical** change. Sometimes this is burning. Petrol is the fuel used in cars. It is burned to provide the energy that makes the car move.

When we eat breakfast the food is the fuel. It undergoes a chemical change (digestion) in our bodies to provide the energy for us to run, skip or even think.

For something to burn you need three things present:

● a fuel   ● oxygen   ● heat

If any one of these is missing then there will be no fire.

You have probably heard about fossil fuels and renewable fuels. At the moment there is great concern about the amount of energy we use and the availability of fuels to provide the energy.

● The fire triangle: if any side is covered up, there will be no fire

● All these are fuels

Look on the CD-ROM to find out how coal, oil and gas were formed.

There are four types of fuel in the pictures. Can you name them? How do we use them? All these fuels need to be burnt with oxygen to release the energy that we experience in different ways.

Just as it is the source of our food, the Sun is the source of all these fuels and in fact of nearly all the fuels we use. Only **nuclear** and **geothermal** energy do not come from the Sun.

26 Make your own cartoon strip to show how coal was made. Make sure you show how the Sun is the original source of the energy in coal. Why is coal called a fossil fuel? What other fossil fuels are there?

27 Suggest two similarities between solar cells and leaves.

Big ideas

Energy stores and pathways

Energetic objects can make things happen and when things happen the energy is shifted from one store to another. So when a girl on a trampoline bounces back up, the energy shifts from the elastic energy store of the trampoline to the kinetic energy store of the girl.

Here is a list of the most common energy stores.

- **Chemical** – in anything that is burning, or undergoing a chemical reaction, including in a battery.
- **Gravitational** – in an object high above the ground.
- **Kinetic** – in a moving object.
- **Thermal** – in a warm object.
- **Elastic** – in a stretched or compressed (squashed) object.
- **Magnetic** – in two separated magnets held near to each other that are attracting or repelling.
- **Electrostatic** – in two electric charges that are attracting or repelling.
- **Nuclear** – released through radioactive decay, fission or fusion.

28 What are the different types of energy in the picture above?

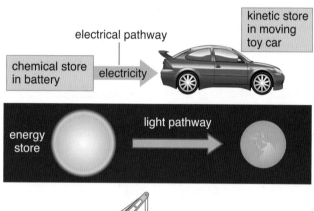

When a battery makes a toy car move we see that energy in a battery (chemical store) is shifted to a moving toy car (kinetic store) via an electric circuit. The carrier or **pathway** for this energy shift is electricity.

Light is another pathway. For example when energy is shifted from the Sun to the Earth it is via a light pathway.

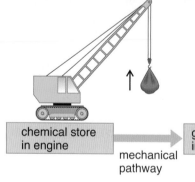

We say there is a mechanical pathway when a force is moved through a distance. For example when a crane lifts a sack of bricks the chemical store in the crane's petrol engine is transferred to the gravitational store of the lifted sack of bricks by a mechanical pathway. We can show this in an **energy flow chart**.

29 Draw an energy flow chart for each action in the table. Look on the CD-ROM if you need help.

Chemical	Gravitational	Kinetic	Thermal
candle burning	rocket taking off	battery powered toy car	heating up supper on the cooker
Elastic	**Magnetic**	**Electrostatic**	**Nuclear**
catapult firing	sorting pre- and post-1992 pennies	charged balloon lifting hair	Sun heating the Earth

Big ideas

4 | Life goes on

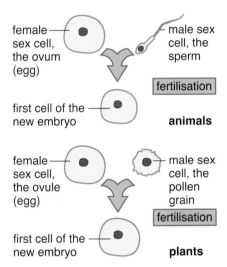

Asexual reproduction in yeast. The parent yeast cell produces small buds that break off to form new yeast cells

Sexual reproduction in animals and plants

Read on the CD-ROM about how egg and sperm cells are adapted for their roles.

The next generation

This chapter is about **reproduction**. Reproduction ensures that the next generation carries on. It is one of the characteristics of all living things (see page 6).

There are two types of reproduction.

- **Asexual reproduction** – there is only one parent and all the offspring are genetically identical. Look back at the diagram of bacteria reproducing on page 8. The bacterium just splits into two new cells. This is an example of asexual reproduction.
- **Sexual reproduction** – there are two parents and each parent produces **sex cells** (gametes) that have to fuse together, mixing the **genes** of both parents in the process of **fertilisation**.

In humans (and most animals) reproduction is **sexual**. This means humans have two parents. The mother produces female sex cells called **eggs** or **ova**. The father produces male sex cells called **sperms**.

Each sex cell carries genetic material on **chromosomes** inside its nucleus.

When the male nucleus and the female nucleus fuse together during fertilisation, the chromosomes are mixed up and a new individual with unique characteristics is made. This first cell of the new individual is called a **zygote**.

1 Explain why a new individual produced from sexual reproduction is never the same as its mother or its father.
2 Explain how the sperm cell is adapted to its role of swimming to an egg and providing the father's chromosomes.
3 Explain how the egg cell is adapted to its role of providing the mother's chromosomes and sustaining the young embryo for a few days.
4 Why do you think a bird's egg is so big compared to a human egg?

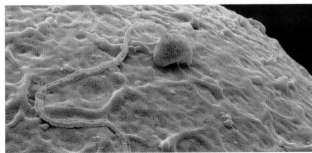

A human sperm entering an egg, seen with an electron microscope

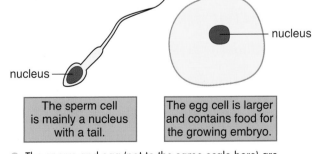

The sperm and egg (not to the same scale here) are adapted to their functions

The sperm cell is mainly a nucleus with a tail.

The egg cell is larger and contains food for the growing embryo.

Life goes on

41

How is sex determined?

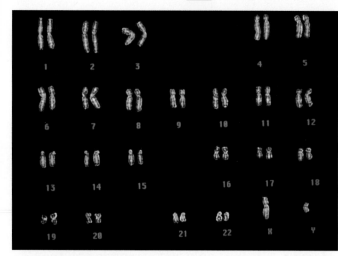

A full set of male human chromosomes

Human body cells contain 23 pairs of **chromosomes** – strands of genetic material. In a male, as shown in the photo, the 23rd pair consists of an 'X' (long) and a 'Y' (short) chromosome. In a female, the 23rd pair consists of two X chromosomes.

In a sex cell (egg or sperm), however, there are 23 *single* chromosomes – one from each pair. So while an egg cell always carries an X chromosome, a sperm cell may carry an X *or* a Y chromosome. When an egg and a sperm join together in fertilisation, it is this 23rd chromosome that determines the sex of the offspring. The diagrams show what can happen.

There is a 50:50 chance of the new cell having an XX pair, and so becoming a girl, or having an XY pair, and so becoming a boy. This is because equal numbers of X-carrying and Y-carrying sperm are produced.

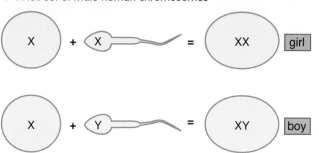

Is it a boy or a girl?

Choosing the sex of offspring

Many farmers want to choose the sex of their animals. For example a dairy farmer would like to produce female cattle, so scientists have developed some techniques for increasing the number of female offspring in farm animals. One such technique spins sperm samples at very high speeds in a centrifuge. Because the female chromosome is very slightly heavier than the male one, more female sperms sink to the bottom of the sample. The top layer is removed and the cows are **artificially inseminated** with the bottom layer of sperm cells. Because the weight difference is very slight, this is by no means a foolproof method, but it can increase the proportion of female cattle born.

Another method involves marking the X and Y sperm cells with fluorescent dyes so that they can be picked out under a microscope. Doctors sometimes make this technique available to potential clients who would like to choose the sex of their child. For example, some fatal diseases are only passed on to male offspring. If parents knew they carried genes for such a disease, they would want to ensure they had a daughter.

5 What reasons other than those given in the text would make a farmer want to choose the sex of farm animals?

6 Do you think a couple should be allowed to choose the sex of their child? Use the web link on the CD-ROM to help you consider this.

Multiple births

Humans usually give birth to only one baby at a time and this is the result of one egg being fertilised by one sperm.

In many other animals and, sometimes in humans, more than one offspring are produced at once. If there are two offspring they are called **twins**. There are two types of twins.

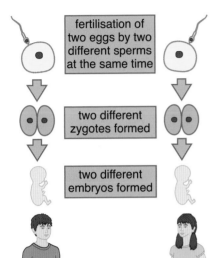

How non-identical twins are produced

- **Non-identical twins** or **fraternal twins** – this type of twins occur when two eggs are fertilised by two different sperms. These twins are no more similar than any other brothers and sisters.
- **Identical twins** – these come from only one egg and one sperm. After the zygote divides into two cells, these split and grow to form two embryos that are genetically identical.

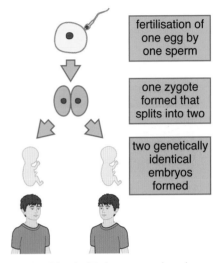

How identical twins are produced

The number of multiple births has increased because of modern **fertility** (often called **IVF**) **treatment**. Doctors use hormones to promote the growth and release of eggs. Sometimes several eggs mature and leave the ovary together. All these eggs may get fertilised because there are always lots of sperms in a sample of **semen** (the sperm-containing fluid that men produce). Also, more women now wait until they are older to have children and the chance of multiple births increases slightly with age.

Ultrasound scans early in pregnancy can show how many babies a woman is carrying. Women carrying multiple babies need to be supervised closely because there are serious health risks to both mother and babies.

The risks include:

- massive weight increase – this makes it very difficult for the pregnant woman to get about
- incorrect diet – mothers need to eat enough of the right proteins and vitamins to ensure the babies grow healthily
- increased chance of high blood pressure, diabetes and anaemia in the mother – all serious medical conditions
- a higher risk of miscarriage
- **premature** births – this means that the babies are born before they are fully ready for birth. They may need specialised **neo-natal** care in incubators.

7 Why do you think most of the babies born as a result of IVF treatment are fraternal twins or triplets rather than identical twins?

8 Work out the different possible types of individuals in quintuplets in terms of identical or non-identical individuals. Explain your reasoning and use diagrams if they help.

Look on the CD-ROM to see an ultrasound scan of triplets developing, and follow the web link to learn about conceiving triplets.

Reproductive organs

The human male and female reproductive systems are shown below. A **system** includes all the organs and structures needed for a particular function, in this case reproduction.

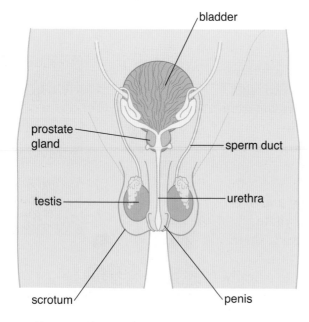

● Human male reproductive system

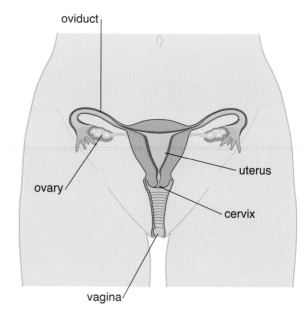

● Human female reproductive system

The table below gives the functions of the different organs in these systems.

Male reproductive system		Female reproductive system	
Organ	Function	Organ	Function
testis (*plural* testes)	Production of spermatozoa (sperms); millions of sperms are made continuously	ovary (*plural* ovaries)	Production of ova (eggs). One ovary produces an egg one month and the other ovary produces an egg the next month
sperm duct (vas deferens)	Transport of sperms to the prostate gland and then to the outside	oviduct (fallopian tube)	Transport of eggs from the ovary to the uterus. Cells lining the oviduct are ciliated and provide wafting movement to move the eggs along
prostate gland	Adds liquid to sperms to produce **semen**, the fluid in which sperms swim	uterus (womb)	Where a fertilised egg implants and grows as a foetus. If there is no fertilised egg, the uterus lining comes away each month during menstruation (a period)
penis	Organ for placing sperms into the female vagina. It contains **erectile** tissue that swells during sexual activity	vagina (birth canal)	The tube from the uterus to the outside. The organ that receives the penis during sexual intercourse. The organ through which menstrual blood and fluids escape
urethra	Tube inside the penis that takes semen to the outside when the penis is erect and urine at other times	cervix	The opening to the uterus at the top of the vagina that is usually tightly closed, but opens (dilates) when a baby is born

● Puberty brings many changes to the body – and mind!

Look on the CD-ROM to learn more about secondary sexual characteristics.

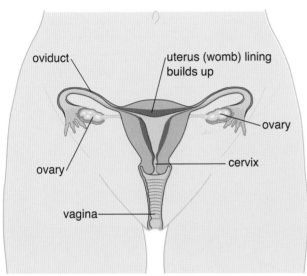

● The lining of the uterus builds up once a month ready to receive a fertilised egg

Follow the web link on the CD-ROM to learn more about ovulation and menstruation and to see an animation of the cycle.

9 Draw up a table to list the changes that occur during puberty. Group these into **Male**, **Female** and **Both**.

Puberty

Puberty is the time when children grow into adults who are capable of reproducing. Some changes, including growth spurts and mood changes, occur in both boys and girls.

All the events of puberty are due to chemicals called **hormones** that start to circulate in the blood. It is hormones that affect behaviour in adolescents, for example causing mood swings. All the changes that happen to our bodies during puberty are called **secondary sexual characteristics**.

Menstruation (periods) in girls

Starting her **periods (menstruation)** is the most significant change that happens to a girl during puberty. It shows that she has begun to release eggs. Every month for the next 30 or more years an egg will leave the ovary (this is **ovulation**) and travel down to the uterus through the oviduct. If sperms are present in the oviduct after **sexual intercourse**, it is likely that the egg will be fertilised. At the same time the uterus is getting ready to feed and nourish a little embryo. Its lining builds up with blood and mucus ready to receive the fertilised egg as it leaves the oviduct. But if the egg is not fertilised, then the uterus lining breaks down and passes out of the vagina with the unfertilised egg in a mixture of blood mixed with watery fluids. This loss is called a **period** and it lasts for 3 to 7 days.

When a girl starts having periods they may not happen every month, but soon they will settle down to a regular approximately monthly cycle, called the **menstrual cycle**. Every woman is different in the number of days the period lasts, the amount of blood lost and the length of the cycle between periods.

During pregnancy, the lining of the womb does not break down and no periods occur until after the baby is born.

Sperm production in boys

Boys know they have started to produce sperms when semen is released from an erect penis. This often happens unconsciously at night (wet dreams).

10 Write about what it would be like to be the opposite gender and going through puberty (i.e. girls write about what it would be like to be a boy going through puberty, and boys write about what it would be like to be a girl).

11 The onset of puberty is celebrated in many human cultures by different traditions and celebrations. Try to find out about some of these.

Conception and contraception

Conception happens when the egg and sperm fuse during fertilisation. It is when a new life begins. For human conception to occur, sperms must be placed into the female's vagina and then swim through the cervix and uterus to the oviduct. A fertile (ready to be fertilised) egg has to be present in the oviduct. Conception is more likely to take place at certain times in the menstrual cycle.

Usually sperms enter the vagina during **sexual intercourse**. They can also be inserted artificially during **artificial insemination**.

Sexual intercourse

When a man becomes sexually aroused he has an **erection**. This is caused by the constriction (tightening) of blood vessels leaving the penis so that the blood cannot leave the penis as quickly as it enters it and the penis becomes swollen and stiff.

Movement between the man and the woman during sexual intercourse causes sudden contractions of the muscles in the penis and sperm duct, sending **semen** containing sperms squirting out (**ejaculation**) into the top of the vagina.

● Coupling during sexual intercourse

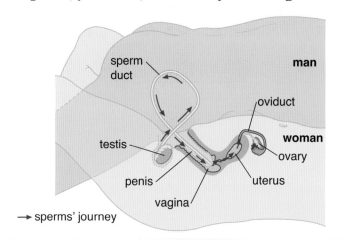

→ sperms' journey

Thousands of sperms pass into the woman in one ejaculation of semen and complete their journey through the cervix to the uterus and oviduct. Some of the sperms die before getting to the oviduct. Only one sperm eventually fertilises the egg.

> **12** Write an imaginative short story about a sperm's journey. Make this story as scientifically correct as possible in terms of the route taken and the structures encountered on the way.

Contraception and birth control

When humans have sexual intercourse they do not always want it to result in a baby. They want to plan when to have babies, so that the baby can be wanted, loved and cared for properly. There are various ways to stop conception and pregnancy. The process of stopping conception is called **contraception**. Different methods of contraception and of preventing pregnancy (sometimes called birth control) are described in the table opposite.

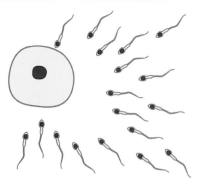

● Many sperms die before reaching the egg and, out of those that do, only one sperm fertilises the egg

A condom ready for use

Contraception/birth control method
Abstinence – not having sex
Barrier methods – include **condoms** (for males) and dutch caps (for females). These should be used with **spermicide** creams because they can split
Contraceptive pill – works by stopping ovulation so that no eggs are released
Sterilisation (called a vasectomy in men) – where the sperm duct or oviduct is cut or tied. This is usually a permanent condition
*Morning-after pill – destroys a newly fertilised egg
*Coil placed in the uterus – stops a fertilised egg from implanting and growing. This has to be placed in the uterus by a doctor

* These methods are not strictly speaking contraception as they do not prevent conception, but they do prevent pregnancy.

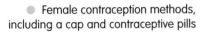
Female contraception methods, including a cap and contraceptive pills

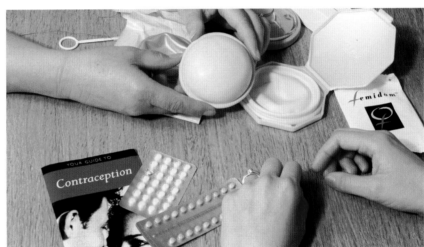

Look on the CD-ROM for more information about contraceptives.

13 Explain how each method of birth control in the table works to stop pregnancy happening after sexual intercourse.

14 Decide which method of birth control you think would be best in the following cases. For each case, state reasons for your choice.

a) A married couple with two children who are not planning to have any more children, but it would not be disastrous and they would be pleased if they did have another child.

b) A newly married couple who want to postpone having a family for 10 years because they want to concentrate on their careers.

c) A young woman who has been going out with her boyfriend for some time, but they have no plans to marry or live together. She is worried because last night they had unprotected sex.

d) A couple who are in a stable relationship but one of them is very concerned about sexually transmitted diseases.

e) Two teenagers who are being pressured by their friends to try having sex even though they both secretly want to wait until they find the 'right' person.

f) A family that has already got four children and cannot cope with any more financially.

Pregnancy

In the first few days after conception, the egg divides into two, then four and so on until it is a hollow ball of cells. During this time the **embryo** moves towards the uterus, where it embeds in the uterus wall (**implantation**).

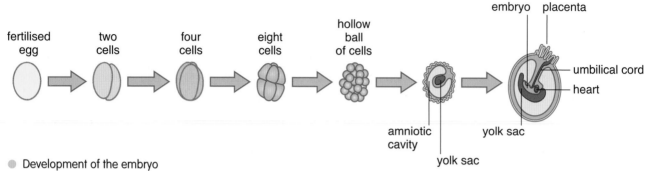

- Development of the embryo

Where the baby fixes to the uterus wall, a new organ called the **placenta** grows. In the placenta, the mother's blood and baby's blood meet, with just a thin membrane separating them. Food and oxygen from the mother's blood pass into the baby's blood. Waste from the baby, such as carbon dioxide and urea, passes into the mother's blood. The **umbilical cord** joins the baby's blood to the mother's blood.

The **amniotic fluid** is a bubble of liquid that protects the baby from pressure from the mother's body and from knocks and bumps from outside. The liquid is contained in the **amnion**.

At 8 weeks all the major organs are formed and the embryo is now called a **foetus**. Pregnancy usually lasts about 38 weeks.

- The foetus and surrounding structures

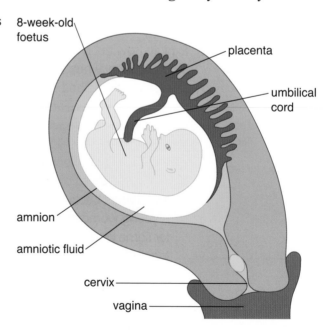

15 Use the CD-ROM to put the pictures of a developing foetus in the uterus into the correct order.

16 What things pass *from* the mother *to* the foetus through the placenta?

17 What things pass *from* the foetus *to* the mother through the placenta?

18 What is the function of the amniotic fluid that surrounds the foetus?

19 After how many weeks does the foetus have all the usual organs and systems of a human being?

20 How many weeks is normal pregnancy on average?

21 Describe the role of the umbilical cord.

A pregnant woman should take care not to allow her personal habits or health to harm her baby. She can protect her growing baby best by eating a good balanced diet, avoiding drugs such as alcohol and nicotine, and keeping fit and healthy.

The table below shows the things that can harm a growing foetus.

Harmful thing	Effect
illegal drugs such as heroin and cocaine	High risk of miscarriage; mother's appetite is suppressed and she may not take enough nutrients for the foetus to grow properly; baby may be born drug-dependent; risk of HIV if injecting drugs and a high risk of passing HIV to foetus
smoking, nicotine	Nicotine is a drug that suppresses the appetite, and smoking inhibits the mother's ability to absorb oxygen. The foetus, deprived of enough food and oxygen, does not grow as well as it should
alcohol	Increases the risks of birth defects, for example heart defects and mental retardation, especially if taken early in pregnancy. Heavy drinking in late pregnancy impedes growth
medications	Medical drugs should only be taken under a doctor's advice; aspirin, ibuprofen, anticonvulsive drugs, anticoagulants and anti-migraine drugs can be harmful to the foetus
some fish contains mercury or other industrial pollutants	Mercury can cause brain damage in the foetus; mercury can collect in fatty fish, for example salmon, tuna, shark, swordfish, bass and bluefish; therefore pregnant women are advised not to eat too much fish
soft cheeses	Some soft cheeses carry bacteria that cause listeriosis, a disease that can cause miscarriage or death to the baby
rubella	This is a virus that can cross the placenta to the foetus; it causes birth defects such as deafness, cataracts, heart defects, liver and spleen damage, and mental retardation, if contracted in the first 3 months of pregnancy. Rubella can easily be prevented with a safe and effective vaccine

Read more about the things that can harm a foetus on the CD-ROM.

22 *Research task:* Using the table above, pamphlets from a doctor's surgery and other information sources, consider what things might harm a growing baby. Produce a web page entry to help pregnant women understand why they need to look after themselves especially well at this time.

Childbirth

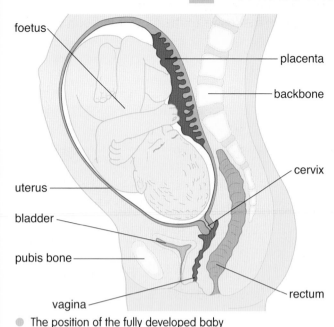

foetus

placenta

backbone

uterus

cervix

bladder

pubis bone

vagina

rectum

● The position of the fully developed baby

Read about the stages of birth on the CD-ROM.

23 What is the advantage of being born head-first?
24 What are the signs that tell a pregnant woman she is about to give birth?

● Childbirth in the 1500s

Follow the link to the web site on the CD-ROM, which gives more information on childbirth in the past and now.

After 9 months, the baby is ready to be born. The normal birth position is head-down (see diagram), although many babies are born feet first.

Birth is caused by the muscles in the wall of the uterus contracting, pushing the baby out. The cervix dilates and gets wider, so that the baby's head goes through more easily. During this process the fluid surrounding and protecting the foetus bursts out ('waters breaking').

Although childbirth is a natural process, sometimes things can go wrong, and women have used the support of other women in childbirth since records began. Women who became expert in assisting in childbirth were, and still are, known as **midwives** – although nowadays men can also take on this role.

From the 17th century, poor women gave birth in hospitals. Initially this increased the number of cases of childbirth fever in women because the doctors did not wash their hands between treating other patients and assisting births. It was safer to give birth at home. Louis Pasteur discovered that the doctors were transferring bacteria on their hands and recommended that they wash their hands and sterilise their instruments before assisting in childbirth. As a result childbirth fever ceased being such a problem. With the added support of doctors and technology, nowadays hospital birth can reduce risks and is considered a sensible option.

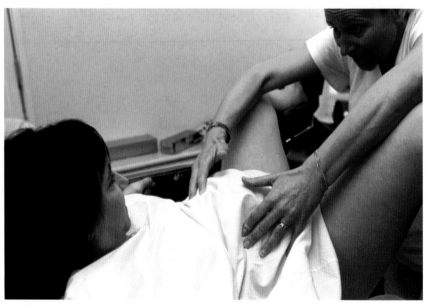

● Modern childbirth

Nowadays pregnant women are surrounded by many professionals to support them through their pregnancy and at the birth of their baby.

Read about working as a midwife on the CD-ROM and follow the links to the web sites.

- **Nurses and midwives** advise women frequently before the birth to ensure that they know what to expect, and when to go into hospital or to call the midwife. They support at the birth and help the mother after the birth of the baby.
- **Doctors** examine pregnant women regularly and do ultrasound scans to ensure the baby is fit and well and growing. They help with the birth if needed, for example if a caesarean birth is necessary – this is when a cut is made in the mother's abdomen (under anaesthetic) to get the baby out.
- **Neo-natal nurses** look after babies who are placed in incubators after being born prematurely (early).
- **Health visitors** visit new parents at home in the first few weeks after birth to ensure all is well and discuss any worries the mother may have.

25 Look again at the information on the CD-ROM about the stages of birth. Draw a flow diagram to show the stages of birth.

26 Find out what birthing was like in the 17th century and what it is like in a modern hospital. Write about the differences.

27 Find out what qualifications you need to train for the jobs in the list above.

28 Write about 'a day in the life of a midwife'.

29 Describe the care needed by babies in the first few months of life.

Reproduction in plants

Flowering plants also reproduce sexually. The flower usually contains both the male and female sex organs, but as these mature at different times, **cross-fertilisation**, where the pollen from one plant fertilises the ovule of a different plant, occurs. The embryo plant receives genes from two different parents (see page 41). The male sex cell is called the **pollen grain** and is produced by the **anther** on the **stamen**. The female sex cell is the **ovule**, contained in the **ovary**, which is part of the **carpel**.

● Grains of pollen on a stigma (×200)

● The female and male parts of a flower

30 What is the difference between pollination and fertilisation?

31 What are the functions of the following parts of a flower?

   petals, anthers, filaments, stigma, sepals

32 How do you think you could artificially pollinate flowers to ensure that pollen from one specific flower is transferred to another? (This is what many market gardeners do to get desirable varieties of flowers.)

Follow the links on the CD-ROM to web sites where you can find out about plant cultivation methods and what it is like to be a horticulturalist (someone who grows plants).

It is the male sex cell that travels to the female one. Plant pollen is transferred to the stigma of a flower by insects or by the wind and the process is called **pollination**.

The pollen grain sticks to the stigma. It absorbs a sugary fluid on the stigma and produces a **pollen tube**. The pollen tube grows down the style of the carpel and into the ovule. The nucleus of the pollen tube fuses with the nucleus of the ovule, fertilisation takes place and a new embryo is formed that grows to become the seed. The seed, when planted and germinated, gives rise to a new plant.

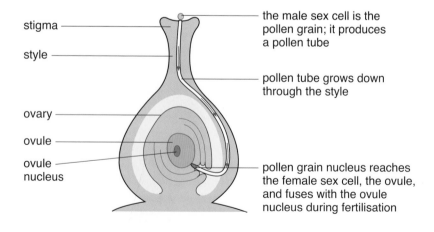

the male sex cell is the pollen grain; it produces a pollen tube

pollen tube grows down through the style

pollen grain nucleus reaches the female sex cell, the ovule, and fuses with the ovule nucleus during fertilisation

● A pollen grain nucleus reaches the ovule by producing a long pollen tube

● Taking a cutting

Some plants can reproduce from **cuttings** (pieces taken from a living plant). This is an example of **asexual** reproduction in plants. Gardeners make good use of this technique to duplicate the same kind of plant or flower. When a plant is pollinated (sexual reproduction), new genes and characteristics are mixed into the next generation. But with cuttings, you know that **identical genes** will be transferred because there is only one parent. So, to be sure of getting what is desired, gardeners take cuttings.

33 Explain why cuttings give exact copies of the parent plant. When is this better than letting a plant produce its own seeds?

34 *Research activity:* Find out which plants are produced asexually commercially – using the techniques of taking cuttings or tissue culture.

Life cycles

A **life cycle** is a diagram that represents the circle of life from one generation to the next.

● Human life cycle

35 *Task:* Try to draw life cycle diagrams for:
  a) a frog
  b) an insect, for example a butterfly
  c) a bacterium
  d) yeast.
  If you need help with the life cycles of the frog and the insect, look on the CD-ROM. See pages 8 and 41 for information on reproduction of bacteria and yeast.

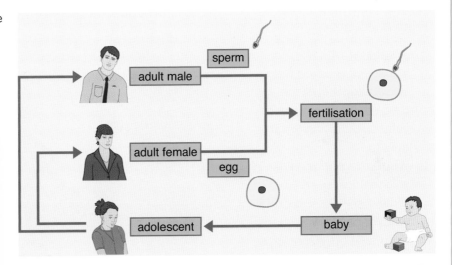

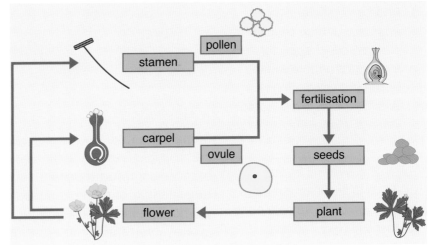

● Flowering plant life cycle

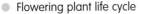

5 Volcanoes

Volcanic hazards

Can you imagine living near an active volcano? Many volcanic hazards are a part of everyday life for the people who live near to a volcano.

Scientists spend a lot of time studying volcanoes. The more they understand about how volcanoes work and what happens when eruptions take place, the more they are able to predict when an eruption might occur and so the more warning they can give to people living near the volcano.

Flows of **lava** from an erupting volcano can be devastating to communities in the area if they have no warning. Hot lava pours out when the **magma** (very hot molten rock) inside the volcano erupts. Large quantities of ash and gases such as sulphur dioxide are also produced in the eruption.

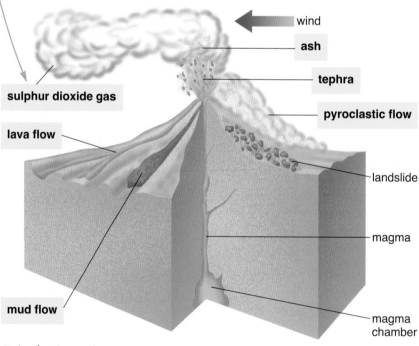

● A volcanic eruption

Sometimes mud flows are created when the rock holding a crater lake gives way. They are one of the deadliest hazards, because communities even a great distance downstream are in huge danger of being engulfed by the rapidly moving mud and debris. The loose rocks produced in landslides can also be a risk, even if a volcano is not erupting.

Look at the diagram on the CD-ROM to learn more about the hazards labelled in boxes.

Follow the web links on the CD-ROM to help you with these questions.

1 A scientist who studies volcanoes is called a **volcanologist**. List the different types of work a volcanologist has to carry out.

2 What different types of volcanologists are there? Write a sentence to explain what aspect of volcanoes each type of volcanologist studies.

3 Find three different university degree courses that you could apply for that would enable you to become a volcanologist. Which A or AS levels would you need to take?

Follow the web link on the CD-ROM to find information about the crater lake on Mount Ruapehu in New Zealand.

Expedition to Mount Kilauea

In 1994 two people standing near the ocean's edge on Hawaii were hit by a sudden wave. They were severely scalded. The water had been heated by lava flows entering the ocean.

Mount Kilauea on Hawaii has been erupting since 1983. The lava flows cover many square miles. New land has been added along the south coast of the island.

Any new active lava flows become popular tourist attractions but visitors can find themselves in highly dangerous situations. Without proper planning, an expedition to the lava flows could prove deadly.

● Tourists visiting a recent lava flow on Mount Kilauea

There is no shade on the lava flows and there are no shops selling supplies! So people are at risk of dehydration, heat stroke, sunstroke and sunburn.

The surface of the lava flows is very uneven, so it is quite easy to fall and sprain an ankle or wrist. Anyone who does fall is likely to cut themselves as the surface can be sharp.

Follow the links on the CD-ROM to read more about volcanoes and safety.

4 a) List the precautions that the tourists shown in the picture have taken.
  b) What do you think the woman with the rucksack should have in it?
  c) Do you think any of the tourists look as if they are not properly prepared?

From lava to rock

If a lava flow on Hawaii reaches a road it just keeps on going. As the lava cools it solidifies to rock and the road becomes impassable.

● A lava flow across a road

● Basalt, a rock formed from lava

5 The Giant's Causeway in Northern Ireland is made of basalt. Use the extra information on the CD-ROM to help you write a short leaflet for visitors. In this leaflet you should describe or illustrate how the landscape may have looked when the causeway was formed and explain the process by which it was formed.

6 Look at this picture of pumice stones and the two pictures on the CD-ROM. Write a short 'life story' of these pumice stones, to explain their texture and why they were found some distance from Mount Pinatubo.

Rocks made from the cooling of molten rock are **igneous rocks**. Those formed from lava that has poured out on to the Earth's surface are called **extrusive** igneous rocks. Lava cools fairly quickly, which gives little time for crystals to grow in the rock. Igneous rocks made from lava therefore usually have only very small crystals. The **basalt** rock formed on Hawaii is a common example of this.

Many of the rocks that make up our landscape today are igneous rocks. This means that a long time ago our landscape was very different – fiery and volcanic – from the beauty spots of today.

Basalt is not the only type of extrusive igneous rock. There are many types of lava, each of which produces slightly different rocks. The same lava can even result in different rocks depending upon the conditions in which it flowed (for example, during an explosive eruption or more calmly).

Examination of rocks in detail can help us to work out the story of their formation. Clues such as the size of crystals or even the lack of crystals can tell us whether the rock was originally lava and, if so, how fast it cooled. Unusual features, such as gas bubbles, can tell us about the eruption of the volcano from which the rock came.

Pumice is an unusual igneous rock. It contains gas bubbles and it floats.

● Sample of pumice from the eruption of Mount Pinatubo (Philippines) in 1991

Investigating lava flow

Lavas differ in the quantities of different chemicals in them. They also differ in how runny they are. The more of the chemical silica there is in the lava, the more **viscous** (thick) the lava is. These thick lavas tend to erupt at slightly lower temperatures.

Experimenting with real lava in the lab is obviously impossible. If we want to find out how the **viscosity** of different lavas affects how fast they flow, we can use other substances to model the behaviour of the lava.

Some pupils decided to use a tray leaning against a pile of books to represent the slope of the volcano. They then chose some different liquids from the kitchen to model the behaviour of the lava. They timed how long it took each 'lava' to flow 20 cm down the slope.

7 The two pictures on the CD-ROM show rocks formed from lava flows. Which picture do you think shows rocks produced by a flow of rhyolite lava and which by a basalt flow? Use the diagram on the CD-ROM to help. Explain your answer.

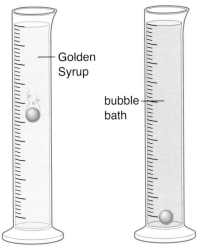

Golden Syrup

bubble bath

● The ball bearing takes longer to fall through the syrup because syrup is more viscous than bubble bath

8 List these substances in order of how viscous you think they are:

treacle, water, cooking oil.

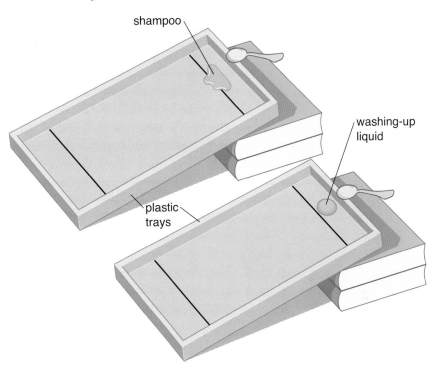

shampoo

washing-up liquid

plastic trays

● Modelling lava flow in the lab

9 Look at the two diagrams of the pupils' set-up. List all the ways that the pupils made the experiment fair.

10 Unfortunately, although they set up the experiment in a fair way, the way they actually did the experiment wasn't a fair test. Look at the diagrams closely. Can you spot what they did that made it unfair?

11 Suggest a way of improving their method that would make their experiment more fair. Use the diagram of useful equipment on the CD-ROM to help you.

Granite – the 'designer' rock

People who are able to have a 'designer' kitchen often opt for **granite** worktops. These are very tough and look attractive too.

● Close-up of granite showing crystal structure

12 Which pot of tea will cool more slowly?

13 Look at the geological map on the CD-ROM. Use an atlas to help you name the places/areas of the UK where granite is found. What does this tell you about the geological past of these places?

14 Look at the pictures of basalt, obsidian and pitchblende on the CD-ROM. Use the information on this page to put these rocks in order of how fast they cooled (starting with the slowest). Explain the evidence for your answer.

Looking at the close-up of the granite, you can see that it is made up of quite large crystals. Compare this to the basalt on page 56. From this we can work out that when the granite formed it must have cooled slowly, in order to allow crystals of this size to grow.

Granite was formed when magma cooled underground. This type of igneous rock is called **intrusive** igneous rock (because it cooled **in**side the Earth). Remember that igneous rock formed from cooling lava is called **extrusive** igneous rock (because it has **ex**ited the ground).

slow cooling   fast cooling

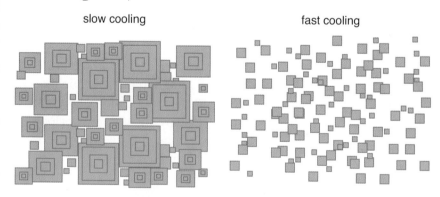

● When molten rock cools slowly there is time for its atoms to arrange themselves in a regular pattern and for the regular crystals to grow before solidifying. When molten rock cools quickly there is no time for crystals to grow in this way. The tiny crystals are embedded in a glass-like material

Rock density

Pumice is a very unusual rock. Unlike other rocks, it floats on water.

● Pumice floats   ● Granite sinks

15 Look at the balance below. Which rock sample is lighter?

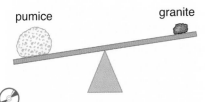

Use the activity on the CD-ROM to investigate these ideas.

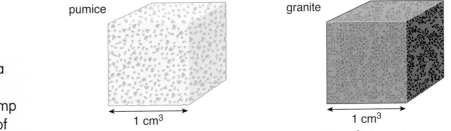

Why does pumice float but granite doesn't?

Pumice is lighter than granite.

It is the size of the piece of rock that is important.

It is not because pumice is lighter than granite that it floats. Pumice floats whereas granite sinks because it is **less dense** than granite – and less dense than water. A piece of pumice is lighter than a piece of granite if you have the same volume of rock.

pumice

granite

1 cm³   1 cm³

1 cm³ of pumice has a mass less than the mass of 1 cm³ of granite

16 A lump of pumice has a mass of 12.8 g and a volume of 20 cm³. A lump of granite has a mass of 26.9 g and a volume of 10 cm³. Work out the density of pumice and of granite.

Density is measured in g per cm³, or g/cm³.

Density = mass (g) ÷ volume (cm³)

Water close up

Look more closely at the water in which the pumice is floating in the picture on page 59. It is totally colourless. We can see straight through it but it is obviously made of something. Water is a liquid that is made up of lots of water **molecules**.

> A molecule is two or more atoms, of *any* element, joined together.

The **formula** of a water molecule is H_2O. This means it is made up of hydrogen (H) atoms and oxygen (O) atoms. A substance that is made up of two or more *different* elements joined together is called a **compound**.

Molecules are often drawn using a circle to represent each atom and using different colours for the different elements. In the diagram of water below, the oxygen is red and hydrogen is white. Obviously atoms are not really these colours – any more than a main road is really red as shown on a map!

18 Subscript numbers $_1$ $_2$ $_3$ $_4$ etc. are used all the time in chemical formulae. Find out how to do subscripts on your computer.

19 The numbers in chemical formulae are very important. Find out the name of the chemical that has the formula H_2O_2. In what way is it very different from water? Give an example of when you would not want to use the wrong one by mistake.

20 Look at the label on a bottle of mineral water. Is it pure water? If not, what other chemicals are dissolved in the water? Find out the symbols for any elements that are in the water.

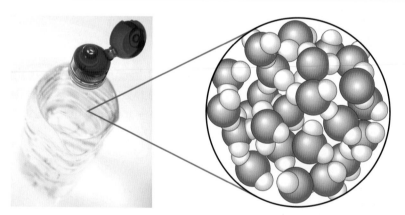

It is water that causes one of the very specific volcanic hazards that tourists must be aware of if trekking on the lava flows of Hawaii. A **tephra jet** is made up of steam and fragments of rock.

21 Draw a diagram to show H_2O molecules in the ocean and then a second diagram of the H_2O molecules after the ocean hits the hot lava flow. Use your diagrams to explain why heating of the ocean water results in an explosive jet of steam. Your teacher may give you a worksheet.

Look at the pictures of different molecules on the CD-ROM.

17 Look at the water molecule in the diagram below. Explain what the small 2 means in the formula H_2O.

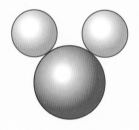

On the CD-ROM there is a picture of a tephra jet and a web link to more information.

Tragedy at Lake Nyos

Look at the interactive map on the CD-ROM showing the position of Lake Nyos.

To learn more about this disaster, follow the web link on the CD-ROM.

On 12 August 1986 about 1700 people were killed by a sudden release of a vast volume of carbon dioxide gas from Lake Nyos, a volcanic crater lake in Cameroon, Africa. All people and animals within a 15-mile radius of the lake died.

● Lake Nyos just after the huge release of carbon dioxide gas in 1986

For some time the exact cause of the disaster was unclear. It is known that a large quantity of carbon dioxide gas was dissolved in the deepest parts of the lake. It is now believed that an event such as a landslide somehow caused the water to overturn. As the pressure decreased, carbon dioxide was released from solution into the air.

A pipe now pumps water from the deepest part of the lake to the surface, allowing the carbon dioxide to be released gradually.

22 Use the formula of carbon dioxide to help you to label a diagram of a carbon dioxide molecule. Explain how you worked out the labels.
23 Think of an everyday use of dissolved carbon dioxide. What can cause a sudden release of this gas?
24 Is carbon dioxide normally deadly? How do you know?

What is carbon dioxide?

Carbon dioxide is not an element. We can tell from its chemical formula (CO_2) that it is made up of the elements carbon (C) and oxygen (O). It is made of more than one element joined together so carbon dioxide is a **compound**.

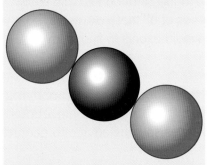

We exhale (breathe out) carbon dioxide all the time. We also enjoy the fizziness it gives to soft drinks.

Carbon dioxide is totally different from the elements of which it is made. Oxygen is the gas we need to breathe in (not out) and carbon is what makes up coal which we use as fuel.

25 What would have happened at Lake Nyos if carbon dioxide had been less dense than air?

To be able to understand why carbon dioxide was deadly at Lake Nyos we need to consider the **density** of gases.

Carbon dioxide is more dense than air. At Lake Nyos it built up in low-lying areas around the lake, with fatal consequences to the local people and their animals. There was no oxygen in the air for people to breathe because the carbon dioxide had sunk and pushed the oxygen higher up out of people's reach.

● The balloon filled with xenon sinks because xenon gas is more dense than air. The balloon filled with helium floats because helium gas is less dense than air

Volcanoes

61

Case study: Long Valley, California

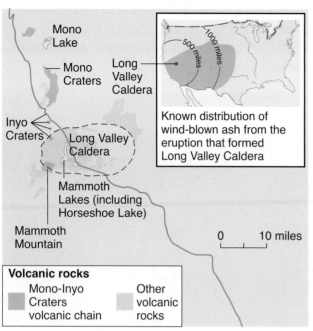

Known distribution of wind-blown ash from the eruption that formed Long Valley Caldera

Volcanic rocks

Mono-Inyo Craters volcanic chain

Other volcanic rocks

Around 760 000 years ago an enormous eruption blew out around 150 cubic miles of magma from under the ground in North America. The Earth's surface there sank by more than one mile. This depression is called the Long Valley Caldera.

You can see on the map that the Mono-Inyo Craters volcanic chain starts at Mammoth Mountain and goes as far as Mono Lake. A series of eruptions about 600 years ago produced more ash and lava flows. Long Valley is famous for its obsidian lava flows.

26 Look at the close-up map on the CD-ROM to see exactly where the Long Valley obsidian lava flows are. Compare with the map shown above. Explain how these flows were formed. Try to include key words from this topic.

27 Look at the chart on the CD-ROM showing the composition of different types of lava. Use the formulae on the chart to list the symbols of the elements that are in the compounds. Use your Periodic Table to find out the names of all these elements. Name the compounds that you would expect to find in lava flows in Long Valley.

Read the US Geological Survey's hazard advice on the area on the CD-ROM.

Around Mammoth Mountain and Horseshoe Lake trees are dying due to high levels of carbon dioxide in the soil. It is a hazardous area and the US Geological Survey gives specific advice to people visiting the area.

28 Use the diagrams on the CD-ROM and your knowledge about carbon dioxide to explain the reasons for the hazards of visiting the area around Mammoth Mountain as described by the US Geological Survey.

29 Look at the small inset map on the map above showing the spread of ash in the volcanic eruption. Work out (approximately) the furthest distance that ash spread. Give an example of somewhere that is this distance from where you live.

Mount Pinatubo

In June 1991 Mount Pinatubo in the Philippines erupted in the second largest volcanic eruption of the 20th century.

● The ash cloud caused by the eruption of Mount Pinatubo in 1991

● Spread of the cloud of sulphur dioxide gas from the eruption

The cloud of ash and gas rose to a height of 22 miles. By one week after the eruption, **sulphur dioxide** gas released from the volcano had reached Africa.

Sulphur dioxide is a compound of the elements sulphur and oxygen. It **dissolves** in water to make sulphuric acid. If the water is the moisture in the atmosphere, then **acid rain** is formed.

30 A diagram of a gas collection method is on the CD-ROM. Explain why this method is *not* suitable for collecting sulphur dioxide.

31 Print out the diagram of the sulphur dioxide cloud from the CD-ROM. Add labels to your printout to explain how acid rain is formed.

Mount Kilauea on Hawaii is another volcano that produces sulphur dioxide. Sulphur dioxide and other chemicals react with sunlight and form **volcanic smog** or 'vog'. This frequently causes problems for local people, as does acid rain (also caused by sulphur dioxide). Problems include difficulties with breathing, reduced visibility on roads, damage to crops, contaminated drinking water supplies, eye irritation and headaches.

32 Out of the problems listed above, make a list of those that are caused by 'vog' and those that are a result of acid rain.

Ready, steady, go

■ Bungee jumping

For many years the word bungy or bungee has been used for the cloth-covered rubber straps with hooks at each end used to keep articles of luggage together. Now, bungee jumping has become one of the most popular thrill experiences of modern times. The first modern bungee jump was made on 1 April 1979 from the 250 ft Clifton Suspension Bridge in Bristol.

Several million successful bungee jumps have taken place since 1980. This is attributable to bungee operators rigorously conforming to standards and guidelines governing jumps, such as double checking calculations and fittings for every jump.

An important property of bungees is that they are **elastic**. Things stretch when a force is applied to them. For example when you pull a rubber band it stretches. In an elastic material the stretching between the atoms causes an opposite force so that when you let the rubber band go it returns to its original length. *Something is elastic if it returns to its original length or shape when any forces on it are removed.* Remember that forces are measured in **newtons** (see page 32).

1 Look around the room. How many elastic objects can you see?
2 Print out the pictures from the CD-ROM of a girl on a trampoline. Discuss with a partner which forces are acting in each of the pictures. Draw arrows on each picture on the printout to show where the forces are acting. In each picture, make larger forces have longer arrows.

Look on the CD-ROM for more information on Hooke's Law.

As you hang weights from an elastic object such as a spring it will stretch steadily with equal increases of the **load** (weight) on it. The increase in length is directly **proportional** to the load on the spring. This is called Hooke's Law.

We can use this property in forcemeters and spring balances for weighing fish, vegetables or even babies, because it is possible to know how long the spring will be when a certain force or **weight** is on it.

In a spring balance it is important that the spring always returns to its original length when unloaded. If the spring is overstretched it will pass its **elastic limit** and will no longer be elastic.

A very useful way of finding out whether an object is elastic is to draw a graph of the extension as the object is loaded.

William and Maya are finding out whether their spring is elastic. If it is, William can use it to weigh the fish he has caught. They load their spring with various loads from 0 N to 10 N. Each time they measure how much it has stretched from its original length. This is called the **extension**.

This is the graph they drew when they plotted load on the horizontal axis and extension on the vertical axis.

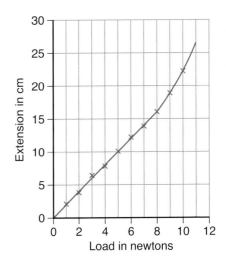

3 How far does the spring extend with a force of 5.5 N on it?

If a spring is behaving **elastically**, the graph is a straight line.

Can you remember what is special about a spring when it is elastic?

4 a) For what load does William and Maya's spring stop behaving elastically? This is the elastic limit. Describe what happens to the extension for each extra newton beyond the elastic limit.

   b) Is this spring suitable for weighing William's fish?

5 William thinks that someone has overstretched the spring in his fishing scales. He puts various weights on the spring and measures its length. Here are his results.

Load (in N)	0	1	2	3	4	5	6	7	8	9	10
Length (in cm)	8.0	10.2	11.9	14.2	15.9	17.9	20.1	21.9	24.0	25.0	28.1

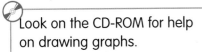

Look on the CD-ROM for help on drawing graphs.

You are going to draw a graph of William's results.

a) Choose suitable scales for load on the horizontal axis and length on the vertical axis.

b) Plot the points using a sharp pencil.

c) Draw the line of best fit through the points.

d) Has William's spring been overstretched? Explain how you have come to your conclusion.

6 Read about the life of a bungee operator and the bungee data on the CD-ROM. The light bungee stretches 1 m for each 5 kg of load put on it.

a) By how much will someone who weighs 75 kg stretch it?

b) If the total drop is 43 m and the bungee is fully extended when the fingers of the person just touch the water below, how long a bungee would you need to use?

c) What energy store increases when the person 'picks up speed'?

d) Why might the bungee 'stretch more than usual' if the jumper is travelling faster?

Ups and downs

This picture shows the **energy stores** that are present in a bungee jump.

Look on the CD-ROM to see more detail of the energy stores at each stage of the bungee jump.

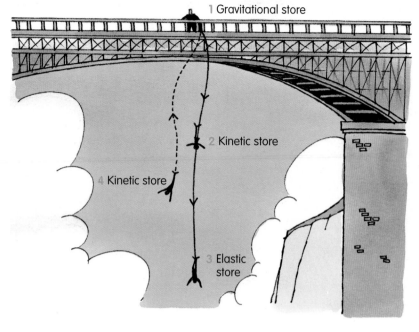

1 Gravitational store

2 Kinetic store

4 Kinetic store

3 Elastic store

I remember! Energy in my gravitational energy store increases when I take off in a plane.

I remember! Something that is moving has energy in its kinetic store.

I remember! When I stretch an elastic band I increase the energy in its elastic store.

The last bit of a bungee jump becomes an oscillation. The person bounces up and down again and again, causing an energy **transfer** from the **gravitational** energy store to the **kinetic** and **elastic** energy stores and back again.

Gradually the bungee system loses its energy to the surroundings and the person comes to rest – hopefully with their nose above the water!

There are lots of examples where energy is shifted back and forth between two energy stores. These pictures show a few.

7 Which of these pictures involve shifts of energy between gravitational and kinetic stores? Explain. Which two pictures also involve an elastic energy store?

● Energy store changes

Off to the fair

This is a painting of a 1920s fairground. Most of the rides would have been driven by steam provided by steam engines. All over the fairground things are happening which involve shifts of **energy** from one store to another.

● The Fairground by Tom Dodson

In the foreground the fair-goers are invited to test their strength to see if they can hit the bell. An energy flow chart for this might look like this:

On the CD-ROM click on the different rides in the enlarged fairground picture to see whether the energy is shifted from a gravitational store to a kinetic store or vice versa.

Kinetic energy store

moving hammer

Gravitational energy store

slider as it hits the bell

8 Read this letter from Fun and Thrills Fairgrounds to Helter-Skelters Unlimited, the slide designers. Using your knowledge of energy stores and pathways, gravity and friction:

a) Plan some experiments to help answer the questions in the speech bubbles.

> What is the best height?

> Does it need humps?

> What is the best surface to help you go fast? Would mats help?

> What is the best surface to stop you at the bottom?

> Is straight or spiral the best shape?

Dear Helter-Skelters Unlimited,

I would like an exciting new adventure slide for my fairground.

Please can your team look at all the factors which would make a good slide and use all the information you gather to give me some ideas for a new slide. I look forward to your report.

Yours faithfully

Fun and Thrills Fairgrounds

b) Draw and label your best design for this slide.
c) Write a reply to Fun and Thrills Fairgrounds explaining why your design is so good.
Think about how you will present the results of your experiments to them.
(Remember to use the words you have learnt in science in your letter.)

Messing about in boats

A cruise ship is very heavy and a coconut shell is very light, but they both float.

How can such different things both float?

9 What would you put in the third speech bubble to help explain why some things can float? Look on the CD-ROM for some ideas.

Whenever an object is put in a liquid, an upward force acts on it. This upward force is called the **upthrust**. For an object to float, the upthrust must be equal to the object's **weight**. In other words the forces must be **balanced**. If the weight were greater than the upthrust, the forces would be **unbalanced** and the object would sink.

Archimedes is famous for finding that the upthrust is equal to the weight of liquid displaced – or pushed aside – by the floating object. So the weight of liquid displaced must be equal to the weight of the floating object.

Find out more about Archimedes on the CD-ROM.

You learnt about density in chapter 5 – see page 59. Look on the CD-ROM to find out more about density and units of measurement.

Density is the mass of $1\,cm^3$ of a substance. It is measured in g/cm^3.

So salty water is denser than pure water.

An object will need to displace less of a dense liquid to support its own weight, so it will float higher.

10 Visitors to the Dead Sea are told that their visit will not be complete without floating in the sea. Anyone can do it. Ordinary seawater has 6% salt, whereas the salt content of the Dead Sea water is 30%. Explain why floating in the Dead Sea is so much easier than in the seas around Britain. You will need to mention upthrust and density.

11 Print out the pictures on the CD-ROM of floating objects.
   a) Draw labels on the printout to show the forces acting on each object.
   b) If the object is floating, are these forces balanced or unbalanced?
   c) If you pushed the coconut further under water, what would happen to each of the forces? Explain what you think the coconut would do when you took your hand away.

● Floating in the Dead Sea

Falling, falling, falling

You may have seen the Red Devils performing at a fete or air show. They are a parachute display team attached to the Parachute Regiment. Each fall includes some freefall time before the parachute opens to allow the jumper to move more gently towards the ground.

A typical jump is made from about 4000 m and lasts about 6 minutes. In the first part the parachutist can accelerate from 0 to 54 m/s in 10 seconds. As long as 45 seconds may pass before the parachute is opened.

Look at these pictures of the three stages in the jump. What forces are acting?

1 Freefall

The parachutist's downward speed increases rapidly

2 Parachute opens

The parachutist's speed increases less quickly now

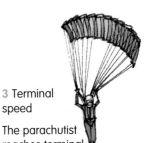

3 Terminal speed

The parachutist reaches terminal (maximum) speed and continues at that speed to the ground

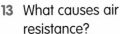

12 Discuss the direction and size of the force arrows for each stage of the jump. See if your partner agrees. Look at the diagrams on the CD-ROM to help you.

13 What causes air resistance?

14 Imagine you are doing a tandem flight with one of the Red Devils. Write an account of your jump including how the forces make you feel at each stage. Your teacher may show you a video of a parachute jump.

Air resistance is caused when air molecules collide with an object going through the air.

So, the more molecules that collide with the object per second, the bigger the air resistance.

So, does that mean that the bigger the area of the parachute, the more the air resistance?

Yes, and the faster the object is moving, the bigger the air resistance.

Water is made of molecules. Is there water resistance similar to air resistance?

15 Using diagrams and the idea of air molecules, explain the physics behind what each pupil is saying.

16 Read the paragraph with gaps on the CD-ROM about diving into water. Fill in the gaps by dragging the words given.

How to run the fastest sprint

We are always interested in **speed**, whether it is to do with the fastest people or animals, or informing us how fast we should travel through towns, or for estimating the time it will take us to get to our destination.

Speed depends on the time taken to travel a certain distance. The formula for speed is:

$$\text{speed} = \frac{\text{distance}}{\text{time}}$$

Typical units of speed are therefore km/h or m/s.

17 Dad says that Alton Towers is about 330 km away and we will be travelling at about 70 km/h. How long will it take us to get there? If we want to be there by 12 o'clock, when will we have to set out?

18 a) Calculate how long it will take the spur-winged goose to fly 100 m.
    b) How far will the eastern grey kangaroo have travelled in the same time?

- Ducks and geese are the fastest birds in level flight. The spur-winged goose can fly at up to 90–100 km/h.
- The fastest kangaroo is the eastern grey kangaroo at 64 km/h.
- The slowest mammal is the three-toed sloth which has an average speed of 0.09 km/h.

- Spur-winged geese

How to improve your sprint performance

When coaches analyse a 100 m sprint race there are three parts of the race that they are looking to improve. The measurement of speed is an important part of this analysis.

- *First stage* – this is the start and first 30 m over which the sprinter should be **accelerating** (getting faster) to their maximum speed. At this stage the **forward thrust** of the athlete from the blocks and from their muscles should be much larger than any **resistance** forces.
- *Second stage* – in this stage the sprinter maintains their maximum speed. The longer they can do this, the quicker they will cover the distance. As the speed is constant, the forces on the sprinter are **balanced** at this stage.
- *Third stage* – the sprinter may **decelerate** or, in other words, their speed will decrease. For maximum performance this decrease should be as little as possible until the sprinter has passed the finishing line. At this stage the forward thrust decreases and becomes less than any resistance forces.

19 Read the section 'How to improve your sprint performance'.
    Draw three pictures of a sprinter, one at each of the three stages. On your pictures, draw and label arrows to show the forces acting.

20 Follow the web link on the CD-ROM to help you suggest ways of:
    a) improving forward thrust at the beginning of the race
    b) reducing air resistance in the second and third stages of the race.

Find out more about instruments used to measure speed on the CD-ROM.

To calculate speed you need to be able to measure distance and time. There are lots of different instruments you could use and you need to choose the ones most suitable for your purpose.

Picture the journey

Sometimes it is useful to have a visual picture of the varying speeds for a journey or a race. Tachocharts are real-life speed–time graphs.

By law the coach driver who takes you on school trips is required to have a rest of 45 minutes after 4½ hours' driving, and a total of 11 hours rest in any 24-hour period. To ensure that this happens, each coach is fitted with a tachometer that records the coach's speed over that period of time. The tachochart is the visual picture of this. It is easy to see how long the coach has been stationary and the speeds at which it has been driven.

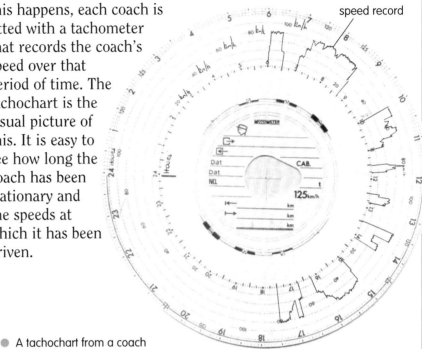

21 Can you see on this tachochart the times when the coach has stopped? The complete circle represents 24 hours. Estimate the total time the coach has been stationary.

● A tachochart from a coach

Speed–time graphs

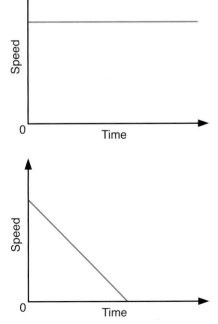

◀ This graph shows an object travelling at a constant speed. It could be a Boeing 747 cruising at 800 km/h.

▶ This graph shows an object starting from 0 m/s and accelerating steadily to a maximum speed. The steeper the **gradient** of the line, the greater the acceleration. It could be a parachutist in free fall.

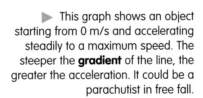

◀ This graph shows an object decelerating steadily to 0 m/s. The steeper the gradient of the line, the greater the deceleration. This could be a car braking steadily until it stops.

▶ This graph shows an object decelerating until it reaches a constant speed. This could be a parachutist from the moment the parachute opened until their terminal speed was reached.

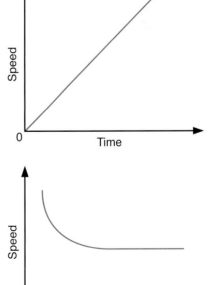

Read more about distance–time graphs on the CD-ROM and follow the link to a web site.

Distance–time graphs

You can also produce distance–time graphs.

22 In the Seoul Olympics in 1988, Linford Christie ran in the men's 100 m sprint and Florence Griffith-Joyner ran in the women's 100 m sprint. The tables below list the times recorded for each of them at 10 m intervals.

● Linford Christie

● Florence Griffith-Joyner

Distance (in metres)	Time (in seconds)	Distance (in metres)	Time (in seconds)
10	1.9	10	2.0
20	3.0	20	3.1
30	3.9	30	4.1
40	4.8	40	5.0
50	5.7	50	6.0
60	6.5	60	6.9
70	7.4	70	7.8
80	8.2	80	8.7
90	9.1	90	9.6
100	10.0	100	10.5

The time interval is the time taken for each 10 m length.

a) Copy the tables and make two new columns. Label the first new column 'Time interval (in seconds)' and the second column 'Speed (in m/s)'.

b) Calculate the speed over each 10 m length using:

$$\text{speed} = \frac{10 \text{ m}}{\text{time interval}}$$

Remember to label the **axes** correctly and to choose a sensible **scale** for your graphs.

c) Draw a speed–time graph for each of the sprinters.

d) Compare the graphs. Say where the two sprinters ran a similar race and where they differed.

Tumblers and tight-ropes

Albert and Albertina are going to Circus School. Here is what they will be learning.

◀ Acrobatic balancing – or, making a human pyramid! It is important to keep the **centre of mass** of the pyramid low and over the centre of the base area.

▶ Unicycling – here they will be practising getting the seat above the wheel quickly. They will then rock the wheel back and forth so that it supports them under their centre of mass.

◀ Tight-rope walking – they will be practising keeping their centre of mass above the tight-rope. If they do not get it right, their weight acting at the centre of mass will make them rotate about the wire and they will fall. Using poles and putting their arms out will help them to balance.

Centre of mass seems very important but what is it?

The centre of mass is the point in an object where all the mass seems to act.

Read about the circus skills of Elfic the Jester on the CD-ROM. Your teacher may show you a video about tight-rope walking.

23 Using the CD-ROM, click on the picture of the human pyramid above. Save it to your computer and print it out. Mark the centre of mass of each person, and where you think the centre of mass of the whole pyramid is.

24 **Stable** objects have a large base area and a low centre of mass. Explain why:
   a) the legs on Zimmer frames for people who have difficulty in walking are widely spaced
   b) many vases have heavy bases that are wider than the necks
   c) wine bottles have thick glass bottoms.

Turning effects or moments

Look at the animation of the clown on the CD-ROM.

25 Can you describe and explain what will happen when the clown continues his walk along the plank?

Find out how a moment is related to force and distance from the pivot on the CD-ROM.

The turning effect of the clown depends on both his weight and how far he is from the barrel. At one end the plank will touch the ground. As the clown moves towards the centre, the turning effect decreases. As he gets near to the middle, the end of the plank will start to rise. The clown can **balance** when he is in the middle directly above the barrel. Here his **centre of mass** is vertically above the barrel (the **pivot**) on which the plank is balancing.

The scientific word for a turning effect is a **moment**.

We have seen that a low centre of mass and balanced moments can help things to balance. Balancing toys use either or both of these.

● Playing with wooden blocks can be a good way to discover about centre of mass and balanced moments – using trial and error!

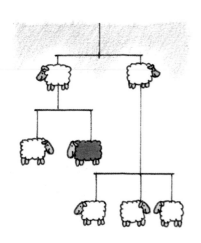

● Mobiles are good examples of a balancing system. Each hanging object produces a moment on the support but this is counteracted by the moment produced by another hanging object

Use these words to help you answer the questions.

stable, centre of mass, pivot, distance from the pivot, moment

26 Your teacher may give you a template like this to make a perching parrot from card. Cut around the outline. Colour your parrot and put Plasticine on its tail.
Now find a perch for your parrot.
a) Why do you need to put Plasticine on the tail?
b) What happens when you tap the parrot's head downwards?
c) Using the idea of a turning effect, explain what is happening.

27 'Weebles' are popular toys with a curved heavy base. The idea is to push them and they will bounce back up.
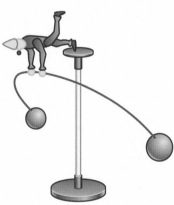
a) Can you explain why they do this?
b) You could make your own weeble with a small rubber ball. Draw a circle on a piece of card and decorate it. Cut a wedge from the circle and curl the remainder so that it forms a cone that will fit on to your ball. Stick the cone on to the ball. You now have your own weeble.

28 This clown can be made to balance and spin on its stand in many gravity-defying and improbable positions. The ability to balance on its nose, toe or hat is due to clever joints and precisely positioned weights.
Explain how you need to position the weights and the clown to make it balance. Remember to use the words you have learned in science in your explanation.

29 Sort the key words from this chapter into groups and make one or several mobiles to put up in your classroom. Your teacher may give you the key words, ready printed, on card.

7 Life and environment

Food chains and webs

In every habitat there are many **food chains**. A food chain describes the feeding relationships and energy flow within a habitat. In the food chain below, the grass uses the energy from sunlight to grow. The rabbit eats the grass and the fox eats the rabbit. Energy passes from the Sun to the grass to the rabbit and finally to the fox.

In a food chain diagram, arrows are always drawn in the direction of energy flow.

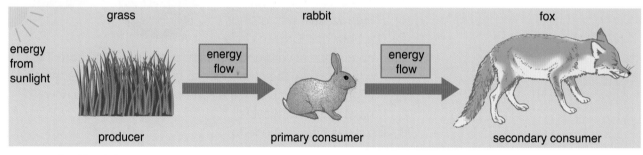

● A woodland food chain

The actual feeding relationships are more complex than a food chain picture shows. The fox does not only eat rabbits. The rabbits are eaten by other animals in addition to foxes. The fairly simple woodland **food web** below shows this. It shows all the feeding relationships between these organisms.

There is a more complicated woodland food web on the CD-ROM.

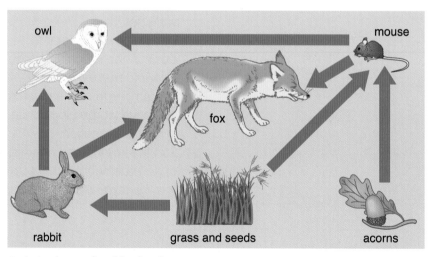

● A simple woodland food web

Most food webs are very complicated. For example look at the pond food web shown below.

● A complex pond food web

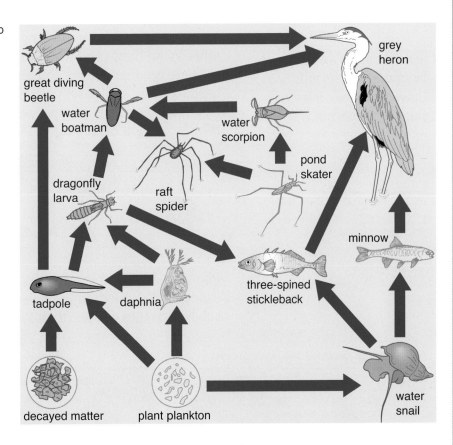

1 Write down as many food chains as you can from the pond food web.
2 This question is about the pond food web above.
   a) Name one producer.
   b) How many different things does a tadpole eat?
   c) Name three primary consumers.
   d) Name two secondary consumers.
   e) Name two tertiary consumers (third-level consumers in a food chain).
   f) Name at least one quaternary consumer (fourth-level consumer in a food chain).
   g) If all the tadpoles in the pond left to become frogs, what would the great diving beetle feed on? How would this affect the population of other animals in the pond?
3 Think of all the wild plants and animals living and feeding in your school grounds (do not include humans). Try to construct a food web to show how they inter-relate with one another.

The variety of life

In a habitat you may find many different kinds of animals and plants living together and depending on one another (for food) and on the environment (for water and shelter). This dependence on other living things and the environment is called **interdependence**.

There are many living things on this planet. Scientists have tried to name and **classify** every different kind of living thing (species) into major groups (called **kingdoms**) based on the living thing's method of feeding and its cell structures.

Read on the CD-ROM about the history of Linnaeus and Darwin and their roles in classifying species.

● Major groups (kingdoms) of living things

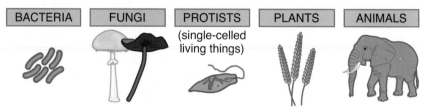

| BACTERIA | FUNGI | PROTISTS (single-celled living things) | PLANTS | ANIMALS |

Plants and animals can further be subdivided into major **groups** called phyla (one group is called a phylum) and these are subdivided into classes, then families and finally species.

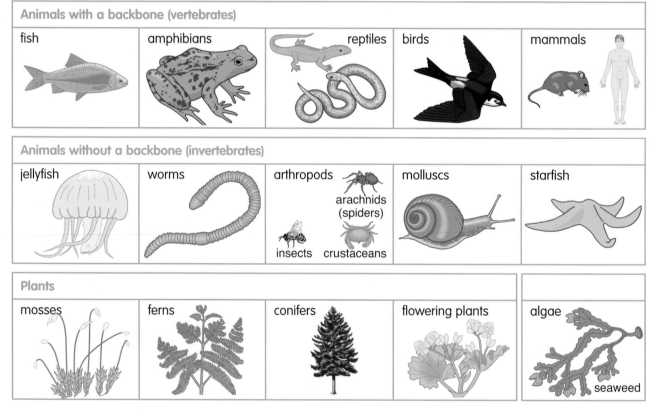

Animals with a backbone (vertebrates)

fish   amphibians   reptiles   birds   mammals

Animals without a backbone (invertebrates)

jellyfish   worms   arthropods   arachnids (spiders)   molluscs   starfish
insects   crustaceans

Plants

mosses   ferns   conifers   flowering plants   algae
seaweed

We can identify living things using a **key**.

4 Look under some leaf litter and try to identify some of the small creatures living there. On the CD-ROM there is a key to animals found in leaf litter.

5 Try to construct your own key to identify the imaginary insects illustrated on the CD-ROM.

Adaptations of plants and animals

Plants and animals are **adapted** to the environment and **habitat** in which they live. Habitats have different **physical factors** that determine what living things can survive there. These include:

- temperature
- rainfall or moisture
- light intensity
- altitude
- topography (for example north- or south-facing).

Physical factors may fluctuate (change) each day or season. For example, in a deciduous forest, daylight hours and temperature are different in winter than in summer. In a desert, days are extremely hot and nights can be extremely cold.

Different species of plants and animals live in each habitat. For example, a forest rat would not be able to live in a desert, but a desert rat has special adaptations that help it survive.

Adaptations in a deciduous forest

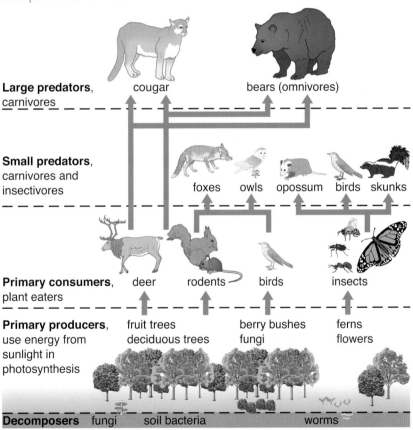

● A deciduous forest food web

Deciduous trees have thin, broad leaves to trap lots of light energy from the Sun for building up food supplies and growth in summer. In winter the leaves drop off and growth stops. This adaptation protects the trees from damage from extreme cold. Many forest animals have **behavioural adaptations**, for example **hibernation** in winter or storing up food (squirrels gather nuts) to get them through winter.

Adaptations in a desert

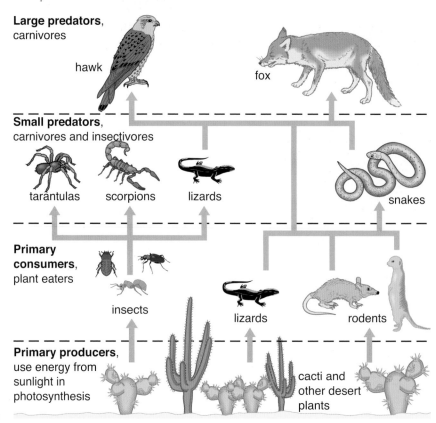

Large predators, carnivores

hawk

fox

Small predators, carnivores and insectivores

tarantulas   scorpions   lizards   snakes

Primary consumers, plant eaters

insects   lizards   rodents

Primary producers, use energy from sunlight in photosynthesis

cacti and other desert plants

● A desert food web

6 Write down some of the physical differences between the deciduous forest and desert environments.

Read more about adaptations on the CD-ROM.

● A desert rat

Desert plants are adapted to a hot and dry environment. Some have very short lives. When any rain falls, they quickly grow, flower and die. Their seeds lie dormant until the next rain, when they germinate and bloom. They grow far apart so that each plant's roots can get water and minerals from a large area. Cacti have no leaves to prevent water loss, just spines to protect them from being eaten by animals. Their chloroplasts are in their green swollen stems where they store water. They have a waxy surface, which also stops water escaping.

Desert animals also have behavioural adaptations, for example limiting their movement in the middle of the day and feeding at night.

7 Look at the picture of the desert rat. This animal does not produce urine. It burrows in the sand. Explain how these adaptations help it survive harsh desert conditions.

8 Choose one desert or deciduous forest animal and find out more about how it is adapted to its environment.

9 How do desert animals get their water?

10 In what way are the spines on a cactus an adaptation to its environment?

11 How do plant-eaters survive winter in a deciduous forest?

12 How are dandelions and daisy plants adapted to living on lawns? Use the information and pictures on the CD-ROM to help you.

Predators and prey

In every food web there are many **predators** – secondary, tertiary and higher-level consumers that feed off **prey**. **Herbivores** are always prey, for example field mice and rabbits. **Carnivores** are always predators, for example eagles and owls. Some animals are both predators and prey.

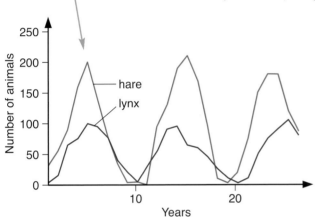

● This bald eagle is a predator

Look on the CD-ROM to see an animated version of this graph with explanatory labels.

13 Name some animals that are both predators and prey. Draw a food web diagram to show this.

There is a delicate balancing act in nature between the predator and its prey, which is known as the predator–prey relationship. It is important that the predator does not kill all of its prey, but leaves enough to survive for a future food supply. When numbers of predators and prey in a particular environment are measured over a long period of time, you can see a graph like the one shown here. There is an association between the populations (numbers) of lynx and hare.

● Lynx and hare

14 Research one other example of a predator and its prey. Write about how each is adapted to its role of predator/prey and how they depend on each other.

There are nearly always more hares (prey) than lynxes (predators). The change in population of the lynx changes in step with the change in population of the hare – its food.

Predators and prey animals have **adaptations** that suit them to their roles.

Predators have features that:

- enable them to find prey, for example good eyesight, smell and hearing
- help them to catch their prey, for example speed of reaction and agility, communication skills (such as teams of lions hunting together)
- help them stun and kill their prey, for example general strength, strong jaws, sharp teeth.

Prey animals have features that:

- help them to hide from their prey, for example good **camouflage**
- help them to notice when a predator is near, for example good senses
- ensure they can escape when being chased, for example by being good at leaping or changing direction
- ensure some of the population survive, for example grouping behaviour in shoals of fish, and herds of cattle.

Human activity and ecosystems – fishing

Fish is a staple food for most human populations, especially in lands surrounded by sea. Fishing is one of the oldest methods of obtaining food. In the past, it did not matter how much fish was taken from the sea – the oceans are very large and there always seemed to be more. Humans were just one of the fish predators.

However, modern trawling methods and technology enable fishermen to take huge quantities of fish at a time. This has disastrous effects on the whole food web. If the prey is removed, the predators will also die. If predators are wiped out, prey populations will increase. The balance of nature will be changed and some species may become **extinct**. Not enough of the food species may survive for future human food.

We need to try to make sure that our fishing methods are **sustainable**. This means that we should only take as much fish from the oceans as can be replaced naturally by the fish reproducing. If we take more than this amount, the fish stocks are **depleted** and our fishing becomes **unsustainable**.

Look on the CD-ROM at the case study of Mallam, whose life depends on fishing, and follow the web link for more information.

Over-fishing causes havoc in the global food chain

Stocks have been hugely depleted in one of the world's richest fishing areas since the 15th century, despite efforts to regulate the fishing industry.

● Trawlers take in vast quantities of fish

Fishing facts:

- 60% of fish in the Southern Ocean has been removed. Whales have become nearly extinct and seals are dwindling due to lack of food.
- Antarctic krill is the food source for an entire web of marine wildlife, including whales, seals, penguins, seabirds, fish and squid. Yet its population is diminishing fast as humans take it for food and industry.
- Globally only 23% of fish are in good condition.
- Over-fishing of cod has caused a decrease in a popular food and an explosion in the crab population in some areas.

Fishing controls:

- Most scientists claim that tougher enforceable laws are needed to prevent further declines. This is a global crisis.
- Enforceable *no-fishing zones* may allow species to recover.
- Many governments have *fishing quotas* (so that only a certain amount can be caught) and *bans on small meshed nets* (so that young fish can escape).
- However, it is difficult to police the sea as it is so vast and much illegal fishing still goes on.

There is more information on krill and human uses of krill on the CD-ROM.

15 Try to work out a food web that links krill, whales, seals, fish, squid and penguins. If you need help there is an example on the CD-ROM.
16 Why does over-fishing of cod cause crab populations to increase?
17 Explain why humans' use of krill threatens wildlife in the oceans.
18 Give reasons for and against Greenpeace's proposal that 40% of the world's oceans should be no-fishing zones.

Human activity and ecosystems – pesticides

A **pesticide** is something that kills pests. Pests are any organisms that destroy human food.

In order to feed the world's growing population, farmers have used pesticides for a long time. The first known pesticide was sulphur dusting in Sumeria, 4500 years ago. In the 15th century, lead, arsenic and mercury (all toxic) were used on crops to remove pests.

Many pesticides are poisonous to humans. DDT seemed very effective and was widely used from 1939 until the 1960s. Then it was discovered that it was found not only in the bodies of insects, but also concentrated in the bodies of their consumers. It ran off into grass and rivers and got into fish and fish-eating birds, and even into cow's and human milk. Toxic pesticides like this, which cannot be removed from bodies, are called **persistent**, as they build up and concentrate through food chains and damage many more living things than the pests they are designed to kill.

Scientists and governments have to weigh up the evidence between the known risks of using or not using pesticides.

Study the pesticide cycle on the CD-ROM that shows how pesticides affect the natural environment.

The CD-ROM shows how DDT can build up through the food chain.

● Farmers have to wear masks and often protective clothing when spraying their crops with pesticide

Arguments *for* use of pesticides:

- Farmers and gardeners need to protect crops from destruction by some pests.
- Without pesticides there would be less food to feed the world.
- Insect-borne human diseases can be prevented.
- Organic produce (without pesticides) goes off much more quickly and is expensive to buy.

Arguments *against* use of pesticides:

- Pesticides are poisonous to living things, and they can get into water systems and food.
- Persistent pesticides continue to build up in living tissue through food chains. They are even present in human tissue and in mother's milk. This will only get worse unless they are banned now.

There is now a worldwide ban on the more persistent pesticides, but debate still rages about the amount of pesticides sprayed on most of our food. Many people are turning to organic food and natural pest control, even though it is more expensive and it is not completely problem free (see page 84).

FEED THE WORLD
BAN PESTICIDES

19 Look at the woodland food web on page 79. Write about what would happen to the animals and plants in the wood if a farmer carelessly sprayed insecticide (pesticide that kills insects) on the wood as well as his field. Show that you understand several consequences of the insects being killed.

20 Suggest reasons why humans use pesticides even when they know this can harm other life in the environment?

Look on the CD-ROM to see what natural methods of pest control there are.

Human activity and ecosystems – sustainable development

As the human population grows ever larger, we use more of the world's resources and space for food and energy. We are destroying many natural ecosystems through farming, pollution and destruction of forests. Future generations may suffer and the very survival of life depends on **sustainable development**:

- not taking more from the planet than we can recycle and give back
- not poisoning the environment
- not upsetting the delicate balance that maintains the great variety of life in our food webs and ecosystems.

There are alternatives to pest control by polluting chemicals.

- Healthy plants grown on healthy soil. Many plants have their own defence systems when not diseased.
- Using other 'friendly' insects or worms as predators of the pest. This is called **biological control**. Ladybirds are native natural predators of aphids (greenfly) and are encouraged into gardens and fields.
- Using homemade sprays based on substances such as dilute washing-up liquid and cooking-oil mixtures.

However, none of these methods satisfactorily meets the needs of large-scale food growers. Scientists continue the search for safe and effective pest control.

Organic farming

Instead of artificial fertilisers, **organic** farmers use crop rotations, natural composting and animal manures to make the soil more fertile. They are not allowed to grow genetically modified crops and can only use – as a last resort – seven of the hundreds of pesticides available to farmers.

Organic animal farming ensures the health of the animal without the use of drugs, and the animals enjoy extensive outdoor grazing. Most organic farms are mixed livestock and crops.

Why do supermarkets sell non-organic food?

- Organic food has not beeen treated with pesticides and preservatives, so its shelf-life is much shorter and it does not always look so perfect. However, it is also energy-efficient because, as it does not keep so long, it is often home-grown and not imported.
- Non-organic food is cheaper because it can be kept for longer.
- However, consumer demand for organic food has ensured that a good range is stocked in most major supermarkets.

Case Study – Harlequin ladybirds

● Native ladybird

● Harlequin ladybird

Harlequin ladybirds were recently brought into the UK on imported plants. They are much bigger than our native ladybird and can threaten its existence. They eat a lot of aphids and breed quickly and attack other insects if there are not enough aphids to eat. Any new animal or plant introduced into an ecosystem upsets the natural balance of any food web.

Read more about the Harlequin ladybird on the CD-ROM.

● Would you buy organic fruit and vegetables?

Read about a career in organic farming on the CD-ROM and the case study of Saway Saiwan, a farmer in Thailand who became an organic farmer.

21 Choose an area for independent study from the following list:

- use of pesticides by a gardener
- use of pesticides by a farmer
- over-fishing by fishermen.

Task: Write a pamphlet from an agency called 'Yes to Sustainable Development', directed at either farmers or gardeners or fishermen, to encourage them to make responsible decisions. Give them guidance about how to do this, for example:

- show them that you understand the reasons why farmers or gardeners use pesticides or why fishermen catch all the fish they can
- explain why using pesticides or over-fishing could eventually damage the very source of their income
- explain food webs and the effects on other living things of eliminating one or two species from a food web
- suggest how to ensure that the ecosystem is not completely damaged.

22 Explain how organic farming is different from non-organic farming.

23 a) Explain the difference between organic and non-organic food.

  b) Why is organic food generally more expensive than non-organic food?

  c) How do you think the government could encourage farmers to grow food organically?

  d) How do you think the government could encourage shops to sell organic food more cheaply?

Acid attack!

All change!

Salt dissolves in water. It does not disappear. If you have ever swum in the sea you may have accidentally tasted that it is still there. All that has happened is that it has broken down into such small pieces that we cannot see it is still there. We can even get it back again by evaporating the water. The salt has not changed into another chemical, so we say there has just been a **physical change**. This change is **reversible**.

If you add a lump of limestone to some vinegar you will produce a lot of bubbles. A new chemical – a gas – has been made. The limestone seems to disappear. You cannot get it back again because it has turned into a new chemical. We say that a **chemical change**, or **chemical reaction**, has taken place. This change is **irreversible**.

● You can see some chemical reactions

1 Two pupils use their knowledge of chemical reactions to build a model volcano. They are using bicarbonate of soda, red food colouring and vinegar. Which of the chemicals will mix with just a physical change? Which two chemicals will produce a chemical change?

2 *Either:* List three types of physical change and one type of chemical change.

Or: Using the CD-ROM, sort the pictures of changes into *reversible* and *irreversible* changes. Then use this to help you write lists of physical and chemical changes.

The acid family

Acids are a very important family of chemicals. We find some acids in our homes; others are used in labs or in industry.

Acids can be very dangerous but by following the correct safety procedures scientists across the world use them every day without coming to any harm.

One of the most dangerous acids is called hydrofluoric acid. It has to be kept in special plastic containers because it reacts with glass. Even so, some scientists do experiment with it. They have to take extra safety precautions including using two pairs of gloves and a face shield as well as goggles.

In the picture below, pupils are investigating what happens when acid is added to rock.

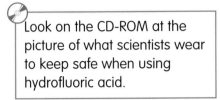

Look on the CD-ROM at the picture of what scientists wear to keep safe when using hydrofluoric acid.

3   a) List the ways the pupils in the picture above are keeping safe when using acid.

    b) One girl has had an accident. How is she making sure that she is not harmed by the acid?

    c) How are pupils making sure their measurement of acids is accurate?

4   Print out the black and white version of the cartoon from the CD-ROM. On the printout, circle all the acids shown in the picture.

Salt and limestone

The scientific name for the salt we eat in our food is sodium chloride. Its chemical formula is NaCl. Salt is a **compound** because it is made from more than one element joined together.

That's what salt looks like close up. The formula says NaCl so it must be like that.

That's impossible. We wouldn't be able to see a molecule that small. I think there must be millions of sodiums and the same number of chlorines.

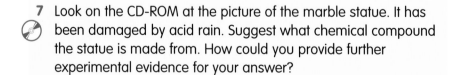

Salt crystals

5 Which of the pupils do you think is right? Explain why. What diagram do you think the second pupil is about to draw?

6 Look at the close-up of salt crystals above. What shape is a salt crystal? Explain why. Look at the salt crystal diagram on the CD-ROM if you need help.

Limestone is largely made up of the compound calcium carbonate. Calcium carbonate has a more complicated formula than salt. Its chemical formula is $CaCO_3$.

You can tell what elements it is made from by looking at the element symbols in the formula: Ca (calcium), C (carbon) and O (oxygen). (*Remember:* each capital letter starts the symbol of a new element.)

When hydrochloric acid is added to calcium carbonate, three new chemicals are made – calcium chloride, water and carbon dioxide. We can write this as a word **equation**:

calcium carbonate + hydrochloric acid → calcium chloride + water + carbon dioxide

7 Look on the CD-ROM at the picture of the marble statue. It has been damaged by acid rain. Suggest what chemical compound the statue is made from. How could you provide further experimental evidence for your answer?

What a reaction!

Chemists experiment to find out what happens when different chemicals are mixed.

Ahmed and Jenny mixed together the different chemicals mentioned in this chapter so far. They wrote down their **observations** (what they saw happening).

You can check on the CD-ROM that you understand the word 'observe'.

	Salt (sodium chloride) – what we observe	Calcium carbonate – what we observe
Water	The salt crystals gradually break down and then disappear	The clear water turns cloudy
Acid	The salt crystals gradually break down and then disappear	Bubbles; the white powder disappears

Another sign that a chemical reaction has taken place is a change in colour. This happens if the new chemical is a different colour from the starting chemical.

● Chemistry can be used to do 'magic' tricks

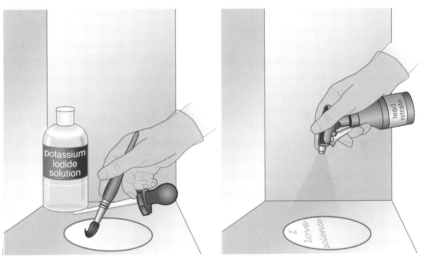

Reactions like this can be used for fun in chemical 'magic' shows but they can also be useful. We'll see next that they can be used as **indicators**, telling us if a liquid is acid or not.

8 Using Ahmed's and Jenny's table, explain what happened for each combination of chemicals. Try to explain as scientifically as you can. You may wish to use words such as:

insoluble, chemical reaction, dissolve, soluble, reversible, irreversible, chemical change, physical change

9 Ahmed and Jenny used the word 'disappear' three times in their observations. Is this correct? Should they use the word 'disappear' when explaining what has happened?

Let's indicate

Acids in foods are often described as sharp or tangy (imagine sucking on a lemon).

The chemical opposite of an acid is an **alkali**. Alkalis were discovered by alchemists in the Middle East as early as the 15th century. The name 'alkali' comes from Arabic.

Most people realise that strong acids are dangerous but strong alkalis are corrosive and can be even more dangerous than acids. One alkali that you will use (well diluted) in the lab is sodium hydroxide solution. The old name for sodium hydroxide is caustic soda. The word 'caustic' means burning. Caustic soda is sometimes used to clear drains. It is harmful and rubber gloves should be worn.

10 Use the pictures below to help you create a list of acids and a list of alkalis. The activity on the CD-ROM may help you answer this question.

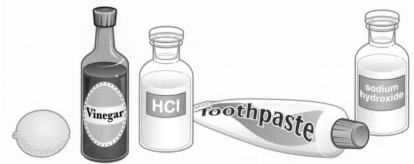

A chemical that changes colour when an acid or alkali is added is called an **indicator**. One of the simplest indicators is **litmus**. It can be used in its liquid form or in paper strips. The table shows you what colour litmus is in acid, in alkali and in a substance that is neither.

11 Natural dyes can be used to make indicators. Name two vegetables that can be used to make indicators. Why is litmus a more effective indicator?

12 Beetroot is preserved in vinegar. Explain why this may make the beetroot more attractive.

	Red litmus paper	Blue litmus paper
acid	stays red	turns red
alkali	turns blue	stays blue
neither acid nor alkali	stays red	stays blue

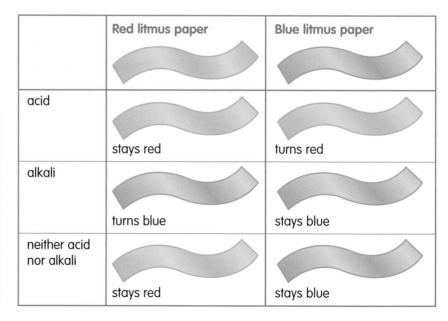

How acidic?

The massive caves at Skocjan in Slovenia were formed as water flowed through the limestone rock. Because the water was slightly acidic, it reacted with the calcium carbonate in the rock, leaving, over thousands of years, a network of caves and passages.

● Skocjan Caves in Slovenia

13 List three places in the UK where there are examples of limestone caves. Explain why they took so long to form. The web link on the CD-ROM will help you.

The water in these caves is not at all dangerous to touch because it is only very slightly acidic. It is useful for chemists to be able to quantify just how acidic (or alkaline) a chemical is. To do this they use the **pH scale**. Strongly acidic substances are pH 1. An alkali is a solution with a pH greater than 7. A substance that is pH 7 is neither acidic nor alkaline – it is described as **neutral**.

● The pH scale

1	2	3	4	5	6	7	8	9	10	11	12	13	14
very acidic				slightly acidic		neutral		slightly alkaline					very alkaline

more acidic   more alkaline

 14 Using the CD-ROM, position the pictures of household substances correctly on the pH scale.

Universal Indicator

The Universe contains all the matter and energy in existence. **Universal Indicator** indicates for all acids and alkalis and tells us how acidic or alkaline they are. Its colour goes from red for the most acidic substances through shades of orange and yellow to green (for neutral) and then into blues and purple to indicate the most alkaline.

Universal Indicator comes with a colour key so that, once you have dipped the indicator paper in the liquid (or added a few drops of the liquid version of the indicator), you can match the indicator paper to the colour key to find the pH.

● Universal Indicator colours

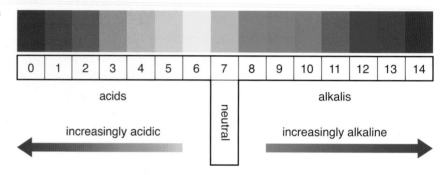

Did you know that we contain acids inside us? The diagram below has been coloured to show the Universal Indicator colour for different parts of the digestive system. (*Safety note:* Universal Indicator should *never* be swallowed.)

● How acid are we?

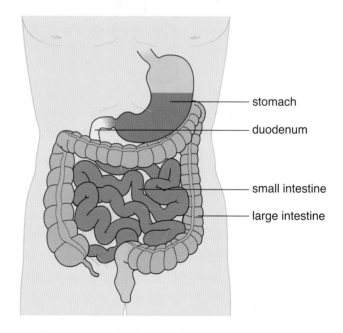

15 a) Use the Universal Indicator scale above to write down the pH of each part of the digestive system. (These pH values can vary slightly from person to person.)
   b) Which part is the most acidic?
16 Vomit (sick) has a pH of 2 (about the same as lemon juice). Explain why this may be.

Neutralise

When an acid is mixed with exactly the right amount of alkali the resulting solution will be neutral. We say that the alkali has **neutralised** the acid. We can test that the acid has been neutralised by using an indicator. The pH should be 7.

Indigestion is caused by an excess of acid in the stomach. Indigestion tablets work by neutralising the acid. Some tablets work faster than others at reducing the level of acidity, and some are more effective than others at fully neutralising the excess acid.

Sarah and Tom compared the effectiveness of three different antacid tablets, A, B and C. They added one tablet of each to the same volume of acid and measured the pH every minute. The table shows their results.

Time (min)	pH		
	A	B	C
0	2	2	2
1	2	2	2
2	3.6	2.8	2.8
3	3.8	3.8	5.2
4	4.2	4.2	5.8
5	4.4	4.4	6
6	4.4	4.8	6.4
7	4.4	5	6.6
8	4.4	5.6	6.8
9	4.4	5.8	7
10	4.4	6	7.2
11	4.4	6	7.4
12	4.4	6	7.6

17 Plot a graph to display clearly the results that Sarah and Tom obtained. There is an Excel spreadsheet on the CD-ROM that you can use to help you.

18 a) Which antacid was the only antacid to totally neutralise the acid? Explain how you used your graph to work this out.

b) Which antacid seemed to start working the fastest? How could you tell this from your graph?

Sarah then added one type of antacid to a test tube containing acid and Universal Indicator.

● An indigestion tablet neutralises an acid

19 Explain these colour changes that Sarah observed.

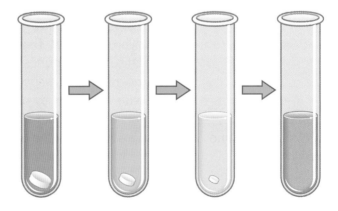

Attacking our past

Archaeologists find out about our past by digging up remains. Sometimes the remains are very well preserved. On other occasions they may have decayed, which means that we can find out less about our ancestors. This can sometimes depend on the conditions in the soil.

● The soil conditions can affect the conditions of remains found at archaeological digs

Fewer remains are found in acidic soils, as the table shows. But even these can tell us a surprising amount about the past.

pH of soil	Typical locations	Remains found
less than 5.5	heathland, upland moors, some river gravels	charcoal; pollen and spores
5.5 to 7	clay valleys and other lowland areas	charcoal; pollen and spores; bones; shells
greater than 7	chalky (limestone) areas, valley bottoms	charcoal; pollen and spores (very rarely); bones; shells

Look on the CD-ROM to learn more about some of the natural remains and how they give us clues to our past.

20 a) What natural remains are unlikely to survive in alkaline conditions?

b) What two types of finds are not found, or may have been damaged, on an acidic site? Explain why.

21 In 2003 Channel 4's 'Time Team' excavated a site in Scotland (Leven, near Fife). The team collected a lot of exciting finds. Of particular importance were some Bronze Age burial chambers. However, most of the human remains had been destroyed. There were also fewer burial goods than expected. Four prehistoric pots did survive.

a) Why do think the human bones had been destroyed? Why did the pots survive?

b) No metal goods were found in the burials. Do you think this means that these people did not have metal goods?

Find out more about the 'Time Team' programme by following the web link on the CD-ROM.

Experiment design

A class was asked to investigate how pH affected the breakdown of bone on an archaeological site. Sometimes scientists use a **model** to mimic the real situation in such a way that they can still draw conclusions that are **valid**. It would be impractical to leave a bone in soils of different pHs to see what happened. It would take far too long to get any results, and getting those results would be difficult.

I am going to use some beakers of different acids.

But that isn't at all like real life. I am going to mix the acid with soil in the beaker.

But how are you going to measure anything doing that? It will have bits of soil stuck all over it!

I could wash it.

22 Which pupil do you agree with? Why?

The pupils decided to use marble in their experiment instead of bone.

23 a) Why do you think the pupils chose marble to represent bone?
   b) In what way is marble similar to bone?
   c) Why do you think the pupils' conclusions would still be valid even with this different material?
24 Your teacher may show you some samples, or pictures, of marble and bone.
   a) In what way is bone different from marble?
   b) How could this mean that the breakdown of marble and bone would differ in the long term?

9 Charges on the move

■ Electricity is all around us

Lisa told Ben that she uses some form of electricity every 15 minutes. Here is her morning schedule.

7.00	Woken by radio alarm clock.
7.05	Hot shower, washed and dried hair.
7.30	Breakfast of cereal, milk from fridge, toast and tea.
8.00	Trumpet practice using an electronic metronome to keep in time.
8.15	Listened to CD of trumpet music.
8.30	Travelled to school, listened to MP3 player on the way.
9.00	In lessons – ICT, English, Science – used computer, DVD player, electronic scales, calculator.
1.00	Lunch: Jacket potato cooked in microwave in the school canteen.

The activity on the CD-ROM will help you find out about different things that use electricity.

1 Can you find 14 uses of electricity in Lisa's list?

Look on the CD-ROM to see the energy flow charts.

In just one morning Lisa has used electricity to provide her with sound, heat, light, entertainment, knowledge and cooked food. The energy stores and pathways involved were thermal, kinetic, light, sound and mechanical.

I don't use much electricity.

But what about your clothes? And your food?

And cars and furniture?

To learn more about the uses of electricity in industry, look on the CD-ROM.

Our clothes, furniture, cars and even the bricks of our houses are all made in factories using machines that mostly are driven by electricity. Food is processed by machines that use electricity. Most buildings are lit and heated, often using electricity.

2 Imagine our world without electricity. How would your daily schedule change?

3 Look at Lisa's morning schedule.
   a) Name two appliances that transfer electricity to thermal energy.
   b) Name two appliances that transfer electricity to kinetic energy.
   c) Name two appliances that end with sound energy.

light bulb

wire

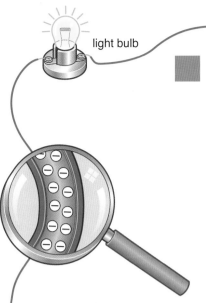

cell

Becoming a circuit expert

As you can see around this page, an electric circuit is a closed loop that contains some important **components**.

- The metal wire is made of trillions of atoms that have loosely bound **electrons** which can move around the wire. Remember that electrons are particles that have a negative electrical **charge**.
- The power supply (sometimes this is a **cell**, or a series of cells which we call a battery, or sometimes it is the mains supply) provides the **energy** to the electrons that gives them a push and gets them all moving in one direction.
- The light bulb **transfers** the electrical energy from the electrons and radiates it as heat and light.
- A **switch** provides a gap in the circuit. When you close the switch the circuit is complete and the charge can flow around it, collecting energy at the power supply and transferring it at the light bulb. The bulb lights at once because there are electrons all around the circuit ready to move as soon as the switch is closed.

An electric **current** is the flow of charge around a circuit. It transfers energy.

Drawing circuits

When an electrician is looking at the electrical circuits in a car or a house, it is far too cumbersome to draw a picture of a battery or a bulb. They use a set of **circuit symbols** to represent various components and a stylised way of drawing circuits as rectangles. Some commonly used symbols are shown in the table.

Circuit component	Circuit symbol
cell	—|⊦—
battery	—|⊦··|⊦—
motor	—Ⓜ—
resistor	—▭—
variable resistor	▱
buzzer	◁
lamp/bulb	—⊗—
on–off switch	—o⌒o—
LED	▷⟋⟋
wire	——

For tips on drawing circuit diagrams look on the CD-ROM.

4 A battery is a collection of individual cells. Explain how adding more cells to a circuit will affect how the electrons move. Will this make the bulb brighter or dimmer? Can you explain why?

5 Draw the big circuit round the page in symbols. You can either do this by hand or electronically, using the web link to the circuit-drawing web site on the CD-ROM. Print your circuit out. Stick your circuit into your exercise book.

6 Draw a diagram of the circuit that may be in your hair dryer.
   a) Where is the original source of energy?
   b) To what other energies is the electrical energy transferred?

7 'Charge is conserved, energy is transferred.' Explain this statement about electric circuits.

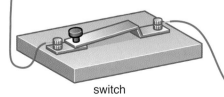

switch

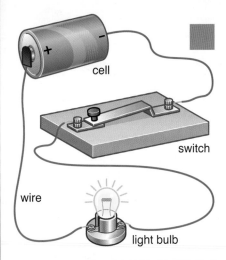

cell

switch

wire

light bulb

Modelling

A **scientific model** is an idea that allows us to create explanations of how we think some part of the world works. Scientists use models because, sometimes, scientific ideas are hard to get their heads around. We cannot 'see' electrons in a circuit, or even the energy transfers, so a model helps us to understand.

One way to model what is happening is to use an **analogy** where we say the scientific idea is *like* something else. Here are two analogies that help us explain what happens when electricity moves around a circuit.

8 a) Which part of the rope analogy symbolises the charged particles (electrons) in a circuit?

b) How do you think the 'bulb's' hands feel? Can you explain this in terms of energy transfer?

c) What would happen to the rope if you had two people being 'cells'? How would this alter how the 'bulb's' hands feel?

- The 'cell' starts to move the rope around in a circle.
- The rope slips through all the children's hands.
- The 'bulb' grips the rope tightly but not so tightly that the rope stops.

● The rope analogy

Look on the CD-ROM for an animated version of

- the rope analogy
- the supermarket analogy.

9 a) Which part of the supermarket analogy symbolises the:
   ● power supply?
   ● bulb?
   ● charged particles (electrons)?

b) How could you use this analogy to explain how the bulb in a circuit could be made brighter?

c) What would happen to the flow of apples if there were two supermarkets instead of one? What would this symbolise in the electric circuit?

lorries deliver apples to the supermarket

each lorry takes the apples to the supermarket

empty lorries go back to the farm to get more apples

empty lorries collect apples at the farm

- The farmer loads the apples on to the lorries and sends them off.
- As soon as the lorries start to move, apples are delivered to SuperFresh, the supermarket.
- All the lorries move at the same speed.
- If the lorries speed up, more apples are delivered to the supermarket in a certain time.
- If the farmer loads more apples on to each lorry, more fruit is delivered to the supermarket in a certain time.

● The supermarket analogy

10 How does each analogy help you to understand:
   a) electric current flow?
   b) transfer of energy in an electric circuit?
   c) the effect on the electric current when more bulbs are added?

In the loop

Series circuits

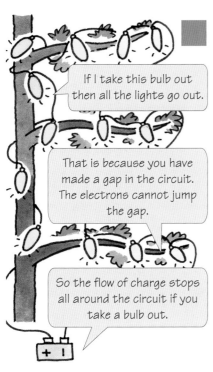

Christmas tree lights are often wired in **series**. The annoying thing you notice about some light sets is that when one bulb goes out all the others go out too and it is very difficult to find the broken bulb.

From the work you have done you should know that:

● circuits need a power supply, wires and an electrical component such as a light or buzzer
● a series circuit is just one loop
● if you increase the number of bulbs in the circuit they get dimmer
● if you increase the number of cells in the circuit the bulbs get brighter
● if there is a break in the circuit then the bulbs go out.

Here are some of the circuits you may have made.

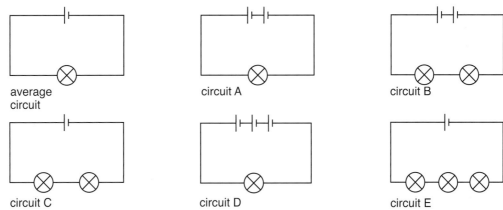

average circuit   circuit A   circuit B

circuit C   circuit D   circuit E

11 Are the bulbs in circuits A to E brighter, dimmer or the same brightness as in the 'average circuit'?

To save electricity in their spaceship, Albert and Albertina want to wire the light over the control panel so that it can be put on at the control panel but switched off at the door. Albert has found two two-way switches like this which he thinks will help.

12 Can you design a circuit that will allow Albert and Albertina to switch the light on at the control panel and off at the door? Your teacher may give you a worksheet to help you.

13 Look at the circuits A to E above.
  a) In which circuit is the bulb brightest?
  b) In which circuit is the bulb dimmest?
  c) How could you adapt the 'average circuit' to test whether a piece of Moon rock conducts electricity?

14 Test your understanding of series circuits with the 'missing words' activity on the CD-ROM.

How big is that current?

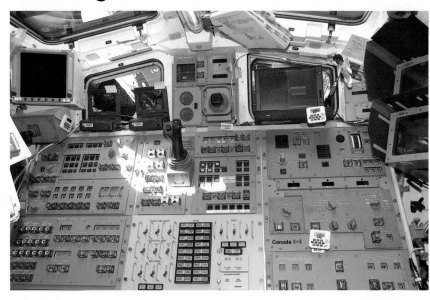

● The control panel in the cockpit of the Space Shuttle

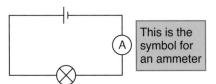

This is the symbol for an ammeter

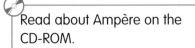

Read about Ampère on the CD-ROM.

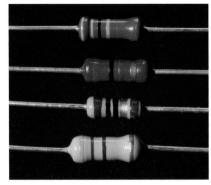

● Different resistors

The Space Shuttle has lots of electrical circuits – to control its speed, direction, temperature, fuel consumption, lighting and heat, to name but a few things. In each of these circuits it is important to know the size of the **current** flowing in the circuit. Each circuit will have an **ammeter** for this purpose.

The ammeter is always connected in **series** in the circuit.

The size of the current depends on the rate of flow of charge or, to put it more simply, the amount of charge flowing in each second. The amount of current flowing in a series circuit is the same anywhere in the circuit. The unit in which we measure electric current is the ampere or **amp** (**A**) for short. It is named after a famous scientist called André Ampère. A current of 1 amp will light a light bulb. About 10 amps are needed to heat the water in a kettle for your tea.

Resistance and resistors

All components such as light bulbs are said to have **resistance**. This resistance slows down the flow of charge and makes the current less.

- A circuit with lots of resistance has a low current.
- A circuit with very little resistance has a high current.
- A circuit with no resistance is called a short circuit and will lead to lots of heat being produced. This is dangerous and should be avoided.

Resistors are specially designed to provide resistance. Most of the circuits in the Space Shuttle have resistors in them so that the right amount of current goes through important components.

15 Do the wordsearch quiz on the CD-ROM that helps you to remember facts about measuring current.

16 What is the current shown on each ammeter display?

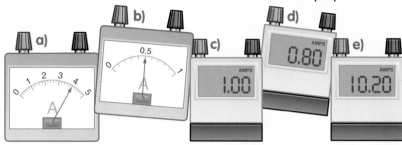

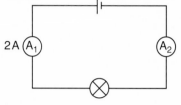

17 a) Angela made this circuit. Ammeter A_1 shows a current of 2 amps. Predict what the current will be through ammeter A_2.

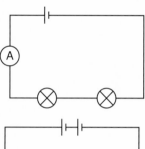

b) She then adds a similar bulb in series with her first bulb. What will be the current shown on the ammeter in this circuit?

c) Amir is going to build the circuit on the right and says that in this circuit the bulbs will be brighter than in either of the previous circuits. Predict what the ammeters will read when his circuit is complete.

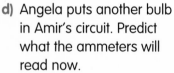

d) Angela puts another bulb in Amir's circuit. Predict what the ammeters will read now.

e) In which of Angela's and Amir's circuits will there be bulbs of similar brightness?

Games and gizmos

You now know enough about electric circuits to make your own game or device. Here are a few ideas.

Flashing badge or T-shirt

You can jazz up your badge or T-shirt with flashing lights.

You need to: Draw a picture or a face on some card. This will be your badge or the face on your T-shirt so you will need to think about what size you would like it to be.

Position some flashing LEDs where you want them in your picture. They could be the eyes of a monster. Connect a circuit so that when the battery is connected the LEDs start to flash. (*Remember:* LEDs need to be connected with the positive (long wire) to the positive terminal of your battery.) Where will your battery be – in your pocket?

Steady hand game

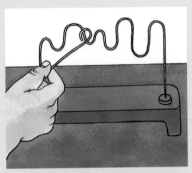

In this game players try to move the loop around a wire without making the buzzer sound (or a bulb light).

You need to: Design a circuit which will be complete when the loop touches the wire. How will you stop the buzzer sounding at the start of the course before the player starts moving the loop?

Alarm your room!

When someone steps on the mat the two pieces of foil touch, making the electric circuit complete, and setting the buzzer off. When the person steps off, the pieces of foil spring apart, the circuit breaks and the buzzer stops. A battery provides the energy to make the buzzer work.

You need to: Design a circuit suitable for your pressure alarm.

Here is a list of the **components** you might need for your circuits:

- cells
- connecting wires
- aluminium foil
- coil of bare wire
- bulbs
- LEDs
- buzzer
- switches
- variable resistors
- ammeter

You will need to draw a circuit diagram before you start.
Now you are ready to start.

- Choose your apparatus and build the circuit.
- Now the important bit ... test it out.
- What will you check if it does not work? This is called problem solving and all scientists and engineers are good at this.
- How about designing some packaging or showing off your invention to your friends?

Read about the day in the life of an inventor on the CD-ROM.

18 You now need to persuade people to invest money in producing your invention. Write a letter to tell them why they should. The CD-ROM gives you some ideas about what should be covered.

19 Try the circuit maze puzzle on the CD-ROM.

Keeping things safe

That bulb is quite hot.

What will happen to the filament if a huge current flows through it?

If more current flows through the bulb it will be brighter and hotter.

● Different types of fuses

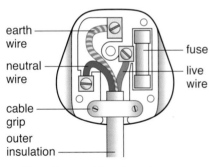

earth wire
neutral wire
cable grip
outer insulation
fuse
live wire

● The wiring and fuse in a plug

To protect a bulb, or other component, from damage if too high a current flows through it we use a **fuse**.

A fuse is a short, thin length of wire that is placed in series in the circuit. If the current gets too large the fuse will melt. This breaks the circuit and the current will stop flowing through the bulb. It is cheaper and easier to replace a fuse than bulbs or even more expensive equipment like computers or televisions.

It is important to always choose a fuse with a current rating that is just higher than the operating current of the circuit.

All household circuits begin and end at the fuse box, which is usually near the electricity meter. The fuses in this box are chosen to suit each circuit. Heating and cooking circuits need a higher fuse rating than lighting circuits.

Modern fuse boxes often contain pop-out circuit breakers instead of fuses. This means that you do not need to replace the fuse each time but the appliance does need to be checked for faults before resetting the circuit breaker.

Appliances have fuses in their plugs. The fuse will melt if the current through that appliance becomes too large. This could happen because of a fault in the appliance, a short circuit or a power surge.

Electricians make sure that houses and other buildings are wired safely.

20 Common current ratings for fuses are 3 amps, 5 amps and 13 amps. Copy the table and choose the correct fuse rating for each appliance.

Appliance	Operating current	Fuse rating
kettle	10 amps	
headlight bulb	3 amps	
hair dryer	3 amps	
TV and DVD player	1.5 amps	

21 Your friend says there is no need for fuses. Explain to him how a fuse would protect his expensive sound system.

Follow the web links on the CD-ROM to read about a day in the life of an electrician and a street-lighting engineer.

Getting hotter

Think of the number of appliances we use every day that are designed to produce heat – hair dryers, toasters, curling tongs, irons, kettles, ovens and electric fires. Each of these has a **heating element** in its circuit.

● These appliances all have heating elements

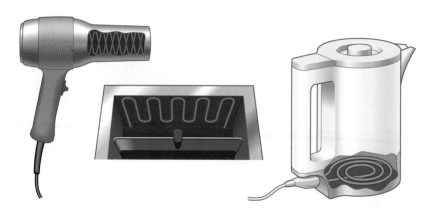

In each of these appliances the electrical energy is transferred in the heating element to radiate as heat.

Heating elements are made of lengths of thin nichrome wire. Sometimes these wires are coiled to take up less space and are surrounded by a metal casing.

Why are lengths of thin nichrome wire used? Nichrome wire is **resistance wire** made from an alloy of nickel and chromium. As its name implies, resistance wire has a high resistance. It will resist the flow of charge through it and transfer energy from the electrons, first to the thermal energy store of the metal and then to radiate it as heat from the wire.

Hot-wire cutters are made from nichrome wire connected to an electrical power supply. When the current flows through the wire, it heats up to about 200 °C. As the wire is passed through the material to be cut, the heat from the wire vaporises the material just in front of it, creating a smooth cut. However, you have to be very careful when using it as the wire is very hot and poisonous fumes are given off by some hot plastics.

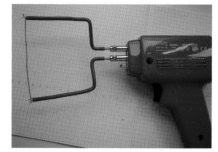

● Hot-wire cutters can be used to cut polystyrene foam

22 Design a cheese cutter using the ideas about the heating effect of electric currents that you have read about on this page. Draw a circuit diagram and explain your design.

23 a) Why is thick copper wire better than thin for use as connecting wires in circuits?
   b) Why is nichrome wire unsuitable for use as connecting wires?

24 An incubator for premature babies has a heating element. The circuit also needs to be carefully controlled with a switch that will cut off the current if the incubator gets too hot. Explain why you think that this circuit needs to be carefully controlled. What needs to happen if the incubator becomes too cold?

Improving performance

All the circuits you have met so far in this chapter have been **series circuits**. Are there better ways of connecting components?

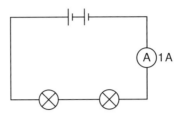

● Series circuit

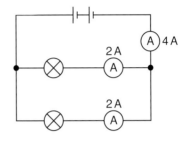

● Parallel circuit

● As you can see, the bulbs in the two circuits have different currents flowing through them. How bright will each bulb be?
● The **parallel circuit** is behaving like two separate series circuits, each with two cells and one bulb.
● Look at the current flowing from the cells in each circuit. You will notice that in the parallel circuit there is more current flowing from the cells than in the series circuit.
● How do you think this will affect the time it takes for each cell to run down? All that energy for brighter bulbs has to come from somewhere and in a parallel circuit the energy is being taken from the cells faster.

What is happening to the flow of charge in the parallel circuit at the top of the page? At the branching of the circuit some charges go into one branch and the others go into the other. If there is the same resistance in each branch, the charges will split equally. This means that the current will be the same in each branch. The current, or rate of flow of charge, to and from the cells will be the sum of the currents flowing through the two branches.

So we can get brighter bulbs by connecting them in parallel but we have to get more energy from the power supply to light them.

There is another good thing about parallel circuits. Imagine removing one of the bulbs from the parallel circuit at the top of the page. You can still trace a complete circuit with your finger from the cells through the other bulb and back to the cell. So that bulb will stay alight. Can you remember what happens if you remove a bulb from a series circuit?

So if the lighting circuit in our house is wired in parallel, the bulb can break in the bathroom and the lights will stay on in the kitchen.

Even to get bulbs of the *same* brightness in a parallel circuit as in a series circuit, more current needs to be taken from the cells. You can 'see' the current flow in the activity on the CD-ROM.

Answer the questions on the next page.

25 Henry's teacher asked what the class thought would happen if she added another bulb:

- in series with the bulbs in the series circuit shown at the top of page 105
- in parallel with the bulbs in the parallel circuit shown at the top of page 105.

a) Draw the new circuits.

b) Here are some of the answers the teacher got. Say which are true statements and which are false.

   1 All the bulbs will be dimmer.

   2 There will be a smaller current in the series circuit.

   3 The bulbs in the parallel circuit will be brighter than the bulbs in the series circuit.

   4 The bulbs in the parallel circuit will break.

   5 The current from the cells in the parallel circuit will be bigger than before.

   6 Only the bulbs in the series circuit will be dimmer.

   7 If you add up the currents in each of the parallel branches it equals the current coming out of the cells.

   8 The current coming out of the cells in the parallel circuit would be the same as the current in the series circuit.

26 Summarise the advantages and disadvantages of parallel and series circuits.

27 Rhys has made this parallel circuit.

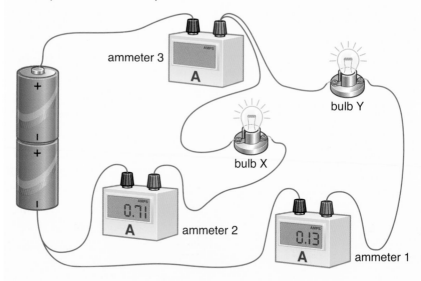

a) How many cells are there in the circuit?

Two of the ammeters are each measuring the current through one bulb.

b) What is the current through bulb X?

c) What is the current through bulb Y?

d) Which bulb will be brighter?

e) How do you know?

f) Which bulb has the bigger resistance?

g) Predict the reading on ammeter 3.

h) Draw the circuit in your exercise book using circuit symbols.

Index

acceleration 32, 70, 71
acids 86–95
adaptations 79–80, 81
air resistance 32, 69
alchemists 20, 21
alcohol 10
alkalis 90
ammeter 100
amnion 48
amniotic fluid 48
amp (A) 100
analogy 24, 98
anther 52
antibiotic medicines 17
artificial insemination 42, 46
asexual reproduction 41, 53
asteroids 28, 29
atoms 24–5, 35
attraction 35

bacteria 6, 8–9, 11, 41, 50, 78
balance 73, 74–5
balanced forces 68, 70
basalt 56
behavioural adaptations 79
biological control 84
birth 50–51
birth control 46–7
boiling point 22
brain 11, 12
Bunsen burner 21

camouflage 81
carbon dioxide 10, 61
carnivores 81
carpel 52
cells, electrical 97
cells, living 6, 11, 13–15, 16
centre of mass 73, 74
charge 35, 97
chemical energy 39, 40
chemical reactions (chemical changes) 39, 86, 89
childbirth 50–51
chlorine 22, 26
chromosomes 15, 41, 42
circuits 37, 38, 97–106

circuit symbols 97
classification 78
colonies of bacteria 8
comets 28, 29
components 97, 102
composter 10
compounds 60, 61, 88
compound microscope 16
conception 46
condoms 47
contraception 46–7
cross-fertilisation 52
current 36–7, 97, 100
cuttings 53

day 30
deceleration 32, 70, 71
deciduous trees 79
decomposers 10, 79
density 59, 61, 68
depletion of fish stocks 82
desert plants 80
differentiation 15
dissolving 63
distance–time graphs 72
doctors 51

egg cells (ova) 14, 41, 42
ejaculation 46
elastic energy 40, 66
elastic limit 64
elasticity 64–5
electricity 36–8, 96–106
electrons 35, 97
electron microscope 7, 16
electrostatics 33, 35, 40
elements 18–26
embryo 48
energy 38, 39–40, 97
energy flow chart 40
energy stores 40, 66–7, 96
equations 88
erection 44, 46
extension 64–5
extinction 82
extrusive igneous rocks 56, 58

fertilisation 41, 45, 46
fertility treatment 43
fields, force 34
fishing 82
floating 68
foetus 48–9
food chains 39, 76–7
food webs 10, 76–7
forces 32–4, 68, 69
formula 60
forward thrust 32, 70
fraternal twins 43
friction 32, 34
fuels 39
function 11, 14
fuses 103

galaxies 28
gases 22, 24, 26, 61
genes 41, 53
geothermal energy 39
gradient 71
granite 58, 59
gravitational energy 40, 66, 67
gravity 33, 34
groups of plants and animals 78
growth 15

habitats 79
hazardous elements 19
health visitors 51
heart 11, 12
heating elements 104
herbivores 81
hibernation 79
hormones 45
host cell 17

identical genes 53
identical twins 43
igneous rocks 56, 58
implantation 48
indicators 89, 90, 92, 93
interdependence 78
intrusive igneous rocks 58
irreversible changes 86
IVF treatment 43

keys 78
kinetic energy 40, 66, 67
kingdoms 78

lava 54, 55, 56, 57
leaves 11, 12
lenses 16
life cycles 53
light microscopes 7, 16
limestone 88, 91
liquids 22, 24, 25
litmus 90
load 64–5

magma 54
magnetism 33, 34, 40
magnification 7
mass 59
melting point 22
menstrual cycle 45
menstruation (periods) 45
mercury 22, 25
metals 22
meteors 29
microbes (micro-organisms) 6, 8–10,
   16, 17
microbiologists 8–9
microscopes 6, 7, 16, 25
microscopic things 6
midwives 50, 51
mitosis 15
models 95, 98
molecules 26, 60
moments (turning effects) 74–5
month 30
Moon, phases of 30
moons 28, 29
multicellular organisms 11
multiple births 43
muscle 11

nanometres 17
negative charge 35
neo-natal care 43, 51
nerves 11
neutralisation 93
neutrality 35, 91
newton 32, 64
newtonmeter 32
non-identical twins 43
non-metals 22
nuclear energy 39, 40
nurses 51

observations 88
orbit 30
organelles 13
organisms 6

organs 11–12
organic farming 84–5
orreries 30
ovary 44, 52
ovulation 45
ovule 41, 52

parachutes 69
parallel circuits 105–6
parallel plate experiment 36–7
parasites 17
pathways 40, 96
periods (menstruation) 45
Periodic Table 23
pesticides 83
pH scale 91, 92, 93, 94
physical changes 86
physical factors 79
pivot 74
placenta 48
planets 28, 29
plant reproduction 41, 52–3
pollen grains 16, 41, 52
pollen tube 52
pollination 52
positive charge 35
predators 79, 80, 81
pregnancy 48–9
premature births 43
prey 81
properties of elements 19, 22
proportionality 64–5
puberty 45
pumice 56, 59

recycling 8, 10
reproduction 8, 41–53
reproductive organs 12, 44–5
repulsion 35
resistance, electrical 100
resistance forces 70
resistance wire 104
resistors 97, 100
reversible changes 86
rocks 56, 58–9
roots 11, 12

salt (sodium chloride) 88
scientific models 95, 98
seasons 31
secondary sexual characteristics 45
semen 43, 44, 46
series circuits 99, 105
sewage 10
sex cells (gametes) 41
sex determination 42
sexual intercourse 44, 45, 46
sexual reproduction 41–52

soil pH 94–5
Solar System 29, 30, 31
solids 22, 24
specialised cells 14
speed 70–72
speed–time graphs 71
sperm cells 14, 41, 42, 45, 46
spermicide 47
stability 73
stamen 52
stem cells 15
sterile techniques 8
sterilisation 8
sulphur dioxide 63
Sun 29, 30, 31, 39
sustainable development 82, 84–5
switches 97
symbols 19
systems 44

tachocharts 71
tephra jet 60
thermal energy 40
time 30–31
tissues 11
tissue culture 15
total magnification 7
transfers of energy 66–7, 97
transplantation 12
twins 43

umbilical cord 48
unbalanced forces 68
unicellular organisms 11
Universal Indicator 92
Universe 28–9
unsustainability 82
upthrust 68

vaccination 17
validity 95
viruses 6, 17
viral diseases 17
viscosity 57
volcanoes 54–63
volcanic smog (vog) 63
volcanologists 54
volume 59

water 26, 60
weight 32, 34, 64, 68

year 30
yeast 10, 11, 41

zygotes 41